Writing as a Small Business

Writing as a Small Business

Nash Black

IF Publishing
Jamestown, KY

The opinions expressed in this manuscript are solely the opinions of the author and do not represent the opinions or thoughts of the publisher. The author represents and warrants that she/he either owns or has the legal right to publish all material in this book.

Writing as a Small Business
All Rights Reserved.
Copyright © 2008 Nash Black
V3.0

Cover Photo © 2008 JupiterImages Corporation. All rights reserved - used with permission.

This book may not be reproduced, transmitted, or stored in whole or in part by any means, including graphic, electronic, or mechanical without the express written consent of the publisher except in the case of brief quotations embodied in critical articles and reviews.

ISBN: 978-1-4327-1625-7

PRINTED IN THE UNITED STATES OF AMERICA

Dedication

To J.C. Conover & James M. Mullikin,
who taught us how to spend money and
traveled with us down a long road. We miss
you.

To John R. Pendleton, PSC,
who routes a new era in our lives.

Table of Contents

Foreword		i
Chapter 1	Start at the Beginning	1
	A. Credentials	2
	B. Death and Taxes	5
	C. Records	6
Chapter 2	Purpose of Records	7
	A. Personal	7
	B. Tax Professional	9
	C. Audits	11
	D. Family and Heirs	14
	E. IRS Requirements	14
Chapter 3	Limits and Sources	17
	A. IF Publishing	17
	B. State Income Taxes	19
	C. Sole Proprietorship	19
	D. Sub Chapter S Corporation	20
	E. Incorporation	20
	F. Resources	21

Chapter 4	Market Research	25
	A. Publishing as an Industry	25
	B. Traditional Publishers	26
	C. Small Presses	27
	D. Private Presses	28
	E. Print on Demand	28
	F. E-Books	29
	G. Anatomy of a Bookstore	33
	H. Readers	37
	I. Money	38
	J. Agents	40
Chapter 5	Keeping Your Records	43
	A. Notebook	43
	B. Computer Spreadsheet	48
Chapter 6	Building Your Spreadsheet	53
	A. Column Designations	54
	B. State Sales Taxes	62
	C. Self-Employment Taxes	75
	D. Supplements to Schedule C	89
	E. Net Operating Loss	94
	F. Withholdings	96
	G. Word File of Procedures	102
	H. Travel/Expense/Activities Journal	108
Chapter 7	Storing Your Records	113
	A. Disaster Preparedness	115
	B. Emergency Measures	115

Chapter 8	Defense, Defense	117
	A. Clean up Your Computer	119
	B. Virus Protection	122
	C. Phishing, Spoof, or Spam	122
	D. Snooper/Spyware	125
Chapter 9	Hitting the Road and Selling	129
	A. Book Signing	130
	B. Credit Cards	131
	C. Travel and Lodgings	134
Chapter 10	Protecting Yourself, Your Family or Heirs	137
	A. Durable Power of Attorney	138
	B. Living Will	139
	C. Wills or Trusts	139
	D. Safe Deposit Box	140
	E. Insurance	141
Appendix I	Self-Employment Taxes	147
Appendix II	States and their Departments of Revenue	149
Bibliography		155
Books		155
Magazines		159
Publishers of Tax Information		160
Websites for Authors		161
Acknowledgments		165
Glossary		169
Index		173

Foreword

Self-employed, under the Internal Revenue regulations, defines an author as the sole proprietor of a small business. A writer is a self-employed professional who is entitled to consideration as a small business under the Internal Revenue Code.

Schedule C of the IRS 1040 is the form for a small business operated as a sole proprietorship. An author is the *sole proprietor* with many functions besides the process of writing. The tax information for *Writing as a Small Business* has been collected for the beginning author. But the same rules apply to any author who files a Schedule C and its supplements with his or her 1040 IRS return.

This volume was developed for following reasons:

1) The major percentage of an author's time is spent marketing his books, which entails expenses not directly related to the process of writing. Writing is a

creative process accomplished within the confines of one's home; hence, it qualifies an author for all the benefits of not only a small business but also the use of his residence as his "tax home."

2) The information contained herein was culled from many sources, as the material referring to authors as a small business, free lancer, self-employed professional, or sole proprietor is scarce. It requires digging and research determination to bring it to light.

3) A professional newsletter suggested that one way to get your name known and sell books is to go on the Internet and establish yourself as an expert in your writing field. We have found that the advice on the Internet is neither reliable nor accurate. When we give you an example or discuss a procedure it has been carefully checked through multiple sources to establish its validity. We do not claim to be experts, but we are knowledgeable about the tax deductions allowable to authors or artists, which they may claim on the Schedule C supplement to the 1040 IRS return.

4) Documentation of each expense and its purpose is the vital element of an IRS audit. Your expense records must support the claims on your return and

establish your intent to sell your writing for an income. You must prepare these records before you see a tax professional for preparation of your individual return.

There are no rules or regulations within the IRS Code that are written specifically for authors. Tax court rulings have favored artists, whose creative occupations meet the same criteria as authors. You must fit yourself into the general rules that govern all small businesses.

5) After our first book, *Taxes, Stumbling Blocks and Pitfalls for Authors 2007*, was published, greater in-depth research flagged several procedures we initially recommended, which were inadvisable. *Writing as a Small Business* is a new title written to comply with current practices, rules, and procedures as they directly relate to authors.
6) Last but not least, when we talk to authors who have been writing for many years about who does their tax returns, their most frequent response is that they give "all of that" to an accountant, a spouse or a relative.

We immediately noticed that the individual had little idea of what is entailed in "all of that." The person who is often cheated is the author not by fraud, but from lack of understanding their work from a commercial point of view. Accountants (and others) cannot work in a vacuum—if the client does not provide the significant information or documentation it will not be included on the return.

Writing as a Small Business is not a definitive guide for tax accounting. It is a method of organizing resources, collecting documentation, preserving materials, and accounting for expenses, which will speed tax-form preparation and provide proof that you are operating your writing career as a small business.

Chapter 1
Start at the Beginning

"**No!**"

There it is—the first line of your book. Bold letters gleam from the page and you are in business.

Yes. You are in business, but not in the way you may have dreamed. You have just become a *small-business entity*, with responsibilities that have nothing to do with writing as a vocation. It doesn't matter if you publish by print on demand, self-publish with a private press, or secure an agent to sell your manuscript to a traditional publisher. The first word makes you a small business from the moment it appears on the page or screen.

This is the point where your life changes. How

you *think* about nearly every move you make becomes important in terms of your writing business.

Where and how will it be sold? What methods will you use to market your production? How you view yourself? How you think about your actions?

How and where will you collect the material to use in your work?

Where do you work?

What are you currently doing that spills over into your work, almost without your being aware of it?

You may have written that "Nick and Nora" were pinned against a ten-foot high wall. How did you rescue them? Did you send a guardian angel on a white horse or was it through their own ingenuity? You, the author, must think of a logical solution.

The same is true of your career as a writer: You must think of each step you take to write and market your work from the standpoint of its being a business.

Do We Know What We're Talking About? Yes.

Our credentials are from both experience and from academic sources.

1) We are the authors of *Qualifying Laps, Sins of the Fathers, Travelers,* and *Taxes, Stumbling Blocks & Pitfalls for*

Writing as a Small Business

Authors, 2007. We have been filing our publishing endeavors with the IRS since the late 1980s.

Writing as a Small Business is more extensive, so it will not become dated until there are major changes in the IRS Code.

2) We were audited by the IRS seventeen times during a period of twenty-two years (1966 through 1988) but never for our deduction claims. In all of those years, the questions were never about the deductions taken but where and when a deduction was included on the forms. One experience was a net-worth audit where the IRS agent came to our home and practically counted the underwear in our drawers—it was that personal and invasive. She took all of our records back to her office and kept them for over a year before declaring they were correct and legitimate. *We never had to pay any penalties or extra taxes.*
3) Because of this frustrating experience with the IRS, I went back to school and acquired majors in accounting, personal finance, and computers to discover what was happening to us and why. The only answer we ever obtained was that in the very early days of IRS computer

development we got stuck like the famous "computer bug" in the Bureau's *new* computer system.

4) For fifteen years I moonlighted at a night school teaching accounting, personal finance, and computer usage. My day job was as a reference research librarian. Over the years I collected two advanced degrees in library science and spent forty-three years practicing my profession before we began our authorship career.

5) 2006 was a disastrous year, when trying to do something right resulted in everything going wrong. We were in the process of creating duplicate copies of files when an auxiliary hard drive (manufactured by IO Magic) self-destructed, abolishing much of our tax information. Everything had to be reconstructed from memory and side trips through accounting texts, IRS and professional tax guides, paper copies of our personal tax-returns, and major help from librarians. http://AskALibrarian.org

We are not certified public accountants (CPAs). That is an area that we do not wish to enter, but what we learned in the "school of hard knocks" can benefit your career and make your documentation of legitimate expenses incurred as an author less of a headache.

Writing as a Small Business

Death and Taxes

In life, death and taxes are two unavoidable events, but you must face only one of them alone. *We do not do our own tax returns*. We use a professional tax accountant. He would be surprised to learn his name is "*indie*" in business jargon, which is an independent business professional. The Golden Rule—*Do unto others as you would have them do unto you*—is the best advice for dealing with financial or legal professionals. Take your records to them in the best manner you can develop. Don't waste their valuable time; after all, you are paying for it.

> "Anyone may arrange his affairs so that his taxes shall be as low as possible; he is not bound to choose that pattern which best pays the treasury. There is not even a patriotic duty to increase one's taxes. Over and over again the Courts have said that there is nothing sinister in so arranging affairs as to keep taxes as low as possible. Everyone does it, rich and poor alike, and all do right, for nobody owes any public duty to pay more than the law demands."
>
> Judge Learned Hand, Helvering v. Gregory,
>   Court of Appeals for the Second Circuit,
>   1934.

Records, records, and more records are your best defense.

The Constitution of the United States does not provide tax deductions. The deductions for which you keep records are a privilege granted by Congress through legislation: the Internal Revenue Code (the Code). These laws are subject to change each time the Code is reviewed.

"Ordinary and necessary business expenses" is the general term for a small business under a sole proprietorship. Your business of writing or authorship must be supported by records to prove those ordinary and necessary expenses.

From the moment you write the first word, start keeping records. It will be a pain, it will cramp your style, and it may even blunt your creativity to develop new habits, but those slips of paper go a long way in supporting your business deductions at the end of the tax year. What we are suggesting is not a "shoe box" method, but it is close.

Chapter 2
Purpose of Records

If we had to rank the four reasons for keeping detailed records, being prepared for an IRS audit would come in last.

Personal. *The first and most important reason to keep records is for your own peace of mind.*

Somewhere, your view of yourself changed. It went from "I want to be an author" to *"I am an author."* Whatever you are doing to support yourself becomes secondary to your writing, no matter when or where you write. You may hear the same phrase (with only slightly different wording) over and over from authors: "It isn't that I want to write. *I must write!"* Keeping records of how you fund your writing career is an organized way to keep a portion of your salary while you're climbing the ladder within the publishing field.

Joe Konrath writes some of the cleverest police procedurals in the business. It didn't happen overnight, but early on, he decided: "*I want to succeed in the business of writing books.*" He knew he had strong stories; he had an agent; and he had sold his work to a traditional publisher. Success? Yes. But he realized that to sell books, he had to make himself and his work known to the public. He had to sell, promote, merchandise, and advertise his "Jack Daniels" mysteries and create his unique marketing style.

> "I didn't get anywhere until I treated writing like a business rather than like winning the lottery. Business requires hard work, dedication and market savvy."
> J.A. Konrath, author of *Rusty Nail, Bloody Mary, Whiskey Sour,* and *Dirty Martini,* writing *for Writer's Digest*, June 2004, p. 35.

Listen to Joe and what he said. Writing *is* a business; it *is* a profession; it *is* a career; and unless you're employed by a newspaper or as a feature writer for a magazine and draw a paycheck, you are an independent self-employed professional in the arena of small businesses. Reporters and feature writers may also have a free lance writing service

Writing as a Small Business

on the side, unless their contract with their employer prohibits such endeavors.

The sole proprietor of your own business. A paycheck and your authorship career may exist concurrently and it should, for the near future. As Joe indicated winning the lottery doesn't happen very often.

Begin to keep records of your travel, paper and ink, phone calls, research, query letters to agents, etc., because these things establish your intent to make a profit, which is used to lower your taxable base from your salaried employment.

Tax Professional. *The second reason to keep records is for the person who will prepare your taxes.*

You can do it yourself, but this is an area like editing. To be "better than good" with your initial efforts, seek help from a professional. You will be glad you did.

If you have questions, write them down so you are not hemming and hawing during your interview. Arrive with expenses listed in reasonable categories; have all of the sums totaled and rounded to the nearest dollar, so that his/her job essentially is to fill in the blanks. This means that you must know why you kept a particular record and know that it is a legitimate deduction.

The person who does your taxes is not your

bookkeeper, and neither is your agent. Many chain tax preparation firms operate under limited liability and will have LLC after their names. They are trained in tax preparation but are not liable in court for the information *you* provide for them. Many people confuse these terms including our editor. Your tax professional may be a certified public accountant (CPA) who is liable for tax information, but the first person who compiles and collects the records and documentation should be ***you***.

A few authors have been so successful with their careers that they have professionals in many areas at their disposal. We have listed them in alphabetical order: accountant, agent, banker, broker, editor, financial consultant, lawyer, media specialist, publicist, secretary, travel agent and tax preparer. Everyone else who has put his or her first words to a medium of communication has become all of the above, rolled into one.

For every individual the scenario is different; for some, a spouse or companion performs part of the functions listed above. But relationships change; being a single parent, supporting children, paying off a student loan, or caring for aging parents are other problems with which many authors must contend. You don't step out of living when you become an author; life will not let you.

Recently, at the First International Mystery Theater Festival, which featured workshops for authors, a young man expressed concern with copyright protection. I mentioned the old method of

Writing as a Small Business

mailing a copy of your manuscript to yourself and placing it, unopened in a lockbox. The presenter called this the "poor man's copyright." Yes, it is, but I've not noticed many independently wealthy individuals taking up writing as a vocation. Our income is limited, and we assume that anyone reading this book also has limited disposable income. *Writing as a Small Business* is intended to help you save both money and major problems.

Walk into a bookstore and compare the number of self-help books available with the number of fiction titles. Bookstores stock books that sell; they are not a warehouses, and neither is a public library. In both realms titles that sit on the shelves collecting dust are of no value. The head librarian and the bookstore proprietor both know that self-help is a major commodity.

Mary Jane Parson's *Managing the One-Person Business* is an older self-help volume that has lists of twenty questions to ask each type of business professional when searching for the one to represent you. One important question, however is missing from the list for a tax preparer/accountant: "Have you ever worked for the Internal Revenue Service as an auditor?"

Over the years, we have found it to be a standard routine that many IRS auditors are serving a personal apprenticeship before establishing firms of their own. Very few of the auditors retire from the IRS. This training is invaluable and cannot be duplicated in an academic setting.

Our first tax accountant was, during the day, the comptroller of Wright-Patterson Air Force Base. With a few simple words, he taught us to never fear an audit: "Have receipts to support every item included as a deduction, and remember that you earn twice what the auditors do. You are paying their salary." He later retired to Florida when the *Busted Flush* was still parked at Pier 17, bought a yacht and setup his own private tax firm, with tax-deductible trips to service clients in the islands.

June Walker's *Self-Employed Tax Solutions: Quick, Simple, Money-Saving, Audit-Proof Tax and Recordkeeping Basics for the Independent Professional* is a current manual with many good ideas for creating your own small-business structure. Many of her suggestions concern changing your way of thinking as a professional with a business intent. At times, she puts information in quotes but does not give a bibliographic source for the quote. We have been able to locate the sources by knowing where to search or how to phrase a question. Her subtitle claims her method is "audit-proof."

We are skeptical of such a promise because the law of averages indicates that over a lifetime of filing tax returns, you are likely to be audited. Due to the sheer volume of tax payers fewer returns are audited each year—estimates indicate about five percent of all returns filed are audited in a given year.

Questions from the IRS are now handled

Writing as a Small Business

through letters of inquiry and it is permissible to give your tax professional the right to answer these questions for you. Tax professionals are also rated by the IRS, and records are kept of the completeness and accuracy of their work. The person whose name is beside yours on the bottom of the return has value against arbitrary audits.

If your records are complete, well documented, and in good order there is no reason to dread an audit. It may be a benefit; we've found that over the years of our engagements, the auditors were exceedingly helpful in pointing out a better means of record-keeping *from their point of view*. There are nuances within the IRS that, completely defy the laws of logic, so from an auditor's standpoint, this is an important consideration.

The real problem is the imposition on your time, which is valuable. An audit is like sitting in a doctor's office; the IRS does not provide remuneration for your time or your loss of salary when you must be absent from your employment.

"You get what you pay for." You are paying in terms of spending a few hours keeping records when you could be writing, so respect your work and time by obtaining the best professional service you can afford. A famous example of carelessness with tax record-keeping was the plight of the country singer, Willie Nelson, who left his affairs in the hands of others. His friends in the music business eventually gave concerts to raise funds to pay off his debt to the IRS.

Hal Advisor, the bar hawk, has ideas for cutting corners, which he is more than willing to explain. Buy him a beer, thank him, and go home to your computer and diligently keep your records for a professional service.

Family and Heirs. *The third reason to keep records is for your family or heirs.*

There are no guarantees that you will be alive or able to file a return for the last year you earned an income, but your estate will be liable to the IRS.

Internal Revenue Service Requirements. *The fourth reason to keep records is to meet the IRS's definitions of legal tax deductions.*

You want to keep more of what you earn. Your records support your claims for expenses and income each year. *They are your documentation of the efforts you have made to write and sell your work*, which establishes your intent to make a profit. They are the major consideration when decisions are made as to your qualifications for inclusion under the Schedule C as a small-business entity.

You must let the IRS know from the beginning that you are an author. It is important to do so and will make your tax life much easier. Your book is a "product" that you are attempting to sell according to the Internal Revenue Code (IRC). Do not be ashamed of the word "product" those who speak disparagingly of a book as a "product" are not aware of the benefits to an author as the sole proprietor of a small business. It's more fun to laugh all the way to the bank when you receive a refund check.

> As an author you are expected to and must prove you have the *intention* of making a profit from your work. This is *marketing* the product for which the expenses are incurred. In today's publishing field very few authors have these expenses paid by their publishers, but they are an essential part of writing and the promotion of your book.

We used our refund check to rewrite *Taxes, Stumbling Blocks and Pitfalls for Authors 2007* and to publish this new title, *Writing as a Small Business.* The first endeavor was a good book as far as it went, but it was lacking in depth and newer insight into the current IRC practices with regard to authors and their expenses. Deeper market research indicated a need for a revision and stronger merchandising techniques. Major changes to a title will cost the author, when using self-publishing, but by the very nature of the method, the author is able

15

to make corrections and withdraw a flawed work from the market. For us the refund check provided a cushion to finance our work.

No one wants one of those brown envelopes (indicating you're being audited) that, arrive in February of the next calendar year for the prior year (or years), especially not when you and your tax professional are preparing the statements for the previous year. Normally, the IRS can go back three years for an audit, but if fraud is suspected and can be proven, seven years is their operating procedure for criminal audits.

Chapter 3
Limits and Sources

If you turn back to the title page of this volume, you will see the imprint: **IF Publishing**. It wasn't until later that we realized "I" and "F" were our initials. The name of the imprint was chosen from the title of Rudyard Kipling's poem.

The IF Publishing imprint was a major reason we chose the publishing package we did from Outskirts Press. Some years ago, we were doing dining-room table publishing of day diaries and cookbooks for a limited sales project. At the time, we filled out the copyright forms and sent two copies of our work, with a check, to the Library of Congress.

We took ourselves seriously, even if the world didn't, so we set up a business entity of publishing costs and income under the name of IF Publishing, using a Schedule C in conjunction with our 1040 tax return. Years passed, and the file was deactivated when we had neither expenses nor income.

Three years prior to the publication of *Qualifying Laps* by Nash Black, we began to incur expenses and a very small income from writing. You are not required to declare income from a source under $400 annually, but you lose the benefits by not doing so and may inadvertently incur a later tax liability. You know the drill for establishing yourself as an author: writers' workshops, submitting writing samples, query letters to agents, professional subscriptions, and office materials. (The only 20th century author to obtain a contract with a manuscript written in pencil on lined paper was Laura Ingles Wilder.)

Income earned, direct sales, advances, royalties, interest and dividends, capital gains, retirement funds, Social Security payments, subsidies, and grants are all income and are treated differently under the IRC. They must be reported to the Internal Revenue Service within the year they occurred. The most famous case of unreported income had to do with Al Capone.

"Wait a minute," your mind jeers, "I take personal deductions without all of this bother." We never took personal deductions of any kind until the cost of health care exceeded our standard deduction. We still don't know a great deal about personal

Writing as a Small Business

deductions or tax credits and will leave those considerations to the experts.

We do not have children, nor do we have the responsibility of financing higher education costs, which fall in the category of tax credits and are outside the realm of our expertise. But there are tax credits available to the small business owner. Talk to your tax professional; some of them may benefit you.

State Income Taxes

State income taxes are not a part of this work. Each state is different, and their procedures and requirements differ from the federal. The *Sister States Tax Directory* offers links to tax information and forms for all 50 states. Visit it at: www.sisterstates.com.

The federal tax structure has consequences for everyone who is a citizen of the United States and earns an income. *Writing as a Small Business,* concerns only a small-business proprietor (**you—author**) with no employees. There are several ways to set yourself up as a business entity.

Sole Proprietorship

The easiest is the sole proprietorship, using Schedule C and its two supporting forms, 8829

Expenses for Business Use of Your Home and 4562 Depreciation and Amortization, plus Schedule E for reporting royalty and other writing income. This is the simplest method and will remain so during the majority of authorship careers.

Sub-chapter S Corporation

A second method is the sub-chapter S corporation, which requires the aid of a lawyer and has many requirements along with the benefit of being taxed on the profits as an individual. At a later date in your professional career it may be worth your time to investigate this avenue, but for now, the sole proprietorship is sufficient for beginning authors. Actually, for most authors the small-business entity is standard, though lawyers and tax accountants may recommend the sub-chapter S procedure.

Incorporation

A third business procedure is to incorporate, but this can be financially dangerous. You may end up paying taxes twice on the same income. A corporation pays taxes, then part of its profits after taxes are distributed to shareholders as dividends. The shareholders then pay income taxes on those dividends. This is what is meant by the term

Writing as a Small Business

"double taxation."

Deductions are not mandatory within the Internal Revenue Code. They are allowed at the discretion of Congress and are written into and taken from the IRC each time Congress rewrites the law. Tax credits are a method that Congress employees to influence the public to take a particular action or to give relief to a portion of the population who have experienced a calamity. Hence, laws may change from year to year or written for a limited period of time. This makes it imperative that you and your accountant both pay close attention to changes in the code and how they affect you, the records you keep, and your financial planning.

There are writers still producing who can remember when the IRC changed for authors. Prior to the change, an author who sold his or her work for a large sum could prorate the income over a period of five years. Prorated income was much easier to live with financially, but this luxury no longer exists.

The major sources for a tax ruling from the U.S. Tax Court and which are quoted in *Writing as a Small Business,* are the publications of Commerce Clearing House. CCH publishes all tax court cases as they occur. Other resources used for tax information are the publications of the J. K. Lasser Institute, *Your Income Tax 2007*, *Small Business Taxes 2007* and *1001 Deductions and Tax Breaks 2007: your complete guide to everything deductible,* published by John Wiley & Sons, Inc. These tax books are the bibles of the tax preparation industry. They have been published for seventy years.

The Ernst & Young Tax Guide for 2007 is a fine professional federal tax manual, which has a reasonable purchase price and is understandable by the general public. The 2007 edition was their twenty-second edition. Their books are different in format and perspective from the J.K. Lasser publications, but all are valuable. We've seen both on shelves in Internal Revenue offices. If it has to do with federal taxes it is in these books—somewhere.

> My father was a treasury agent; he sold a small farm on a land-contract. He wanted to know how to declare the income and in what manner. He had three types of income from the monthly payment: capital gains on his investment, a return of the principal, and interest on the indebtedness. He wrote the IRS asking for help and received several of their publications. He read them, applied a red pen to correct the grammar and returned them, requesting an audit so his question could be answered. His boss chose to ignore him and did not reply. We were delighted when the buyers chose to pay off the loan at his death. Imagine filing state estate taxes for twenty-years—nightmare in spades.

Writing as a Small Business

The government printing office publishes many tax manuals dealing with specific issues and provides instructions with each form. These are available online or from a government depository library housed in many university libraries. Check the websites at the end of this volume; the University of Illinois Chicago houses an extensive collection of tax manuals.

A complete list of all books and publications we consulted are listed in the bibliography. We do not quote from the books we have used because we do not have the author's permission to do so. But we will give you the title of the volume and page number for reference.

Remember that accountants and auditors do not think in the same terms that you do. Their language can be almost as incomprehensible as that of professional computer programmers or insurance underwriters. So try to think in their language. *Lasser's Your Income Tax 2007* has an excellent glossary beginning on p. 779. The glossary of *Ernst & Young* starts on page 733.

What we have attempted to do is similar to reducing a fraction to the lowest common dominator. As time evolves, your record-keeping may need more sophisticated methods, but as a beginner this system will serve your needs at a low cost.

Chapter 4
Market Research

This business activity is called market research under IRS rules, and some expenses can be deducted.

What is the current state of the industry?

When you establish a business, it is a good idea to investigate the industry. You need to know something about your medium of distribution for your product. *Writer's Market* is a good place to begin; the little articles interspersed within the listings will give you a general idea of the industry. *Writer's Digest*, on occasion, over the past 12 years of our subscription, has had articles by persons working inside the industry.

There are two major economic factors rocking publishing today, *over production, with emphasis on an obsolete format* and *technology*. What will emerge ten years, five years, or even by the time this volume is published is not open to speculation. Change will occur—major changes—as the current state of flux cannot continue within any economic system.

Traditional Publishers

The number of major publishing giants producing books in the today, is down to six (or possibly five), only two of which are owned and operated within the U.S. Oops! Limited outlets for your book. These houses do have smaller imprints within their corporation, which are well known in their own right so do not become discouraged by the consolidation of a once-flourishing industry.

Author James Patterson has helped several young authors achieve publication, but it is his "name" which puts his book on the best-seller list. Patterson, King, Grafton, and Burke are brand names, just like Colgate or Kleenex. Their names alone sell the product, and it goes without saying that these authors work very hard to maintain the quality of their books. Time after time they deliver a good read. Anyone can name several excellent authors who were not so meticulous with their product who watched their careers fade. The word in the trade is "an author is only as good as his last book."

Small Presses

Small independent presses are popping up all over the county; these purchase your product much like the traditional major publishers. This growth has been in response to the demand from authors who do not have the "name" recognition that guarantees a best seller and therefore are excluded from consideration by the big houses.

Statistics from the Small Business Administration indicate that of all small businesses that startup within a given year, 85 percent of them fail within three years. Small presses are especially vulnerable, because if the titles they purchased and published do not sell, they cannot purchase other titles; often, they declare bankruptcy.

Any author whose book is owned by the defunct press loses his title and seldom can it be reclaimed, no matter what the market may later be for the book. The same is true if the small press is acquired by a larger company and the author's work is dropped by the parent company. The company still owns the rights to the book, not the author.

Private Presses

Private presses (vanity presses) have been around for many years, but they are a small niche in the total industry. They, too, have changed in their style and offerings. This is an excellent medium for publication of a volume you know will only have a limited regional appeal. The author purchases the entire print-run and then markets her product.

From this point on we will refer to this type of publishing as "private presses," as it is time to remove the negative connotations from this method of publishing, which serves a valuable function within the total industry.

Print on Demand (POD)

Formerly considered an "upstart," POD has changed the industry forever. Some of these entities have been acquired by the traditional publishers or by other concerns because this is the way publishing will be going in the future. (For instance, Amazon owns iUniverse.) It makes sound economic sense. Jobs will be lost and new positions created as the changes are made.

Is POD a publisher or a method of printing? It is both, but in general POD refers to firms like Outskirts Press or others working in this field. Author Mark Levine examines and compares POD publishers in *The Fine Print of Self-Publishing: the*

Contract & Services of 48 Major Self-Publishing Companies.

In the *Novel Writer's Toolkit (2003, p. 219)* Bob Mayer humorously noted that bookstores may someday have a machine in their backrooms that can print a book while the customer waits.

The following is a quote from the New York Times by way of the American Library Association.

> "On August 1, in the lobby of a midtown branch of the New York Public Library, three visitors—a graduate student, a Hong Kong publishing executive, and a sixth grade student—stood in various states of awe as a Rube Goldberg contraption produced a book from digital code to hefty paperback in under 15 minutes. The machine is a demonstration of On Demand Books. . . ." August 2, 2007.

Four years later Mr. Mayer's speculation is reality. A small illustration of how fast the world of publishing is changing to meet new and ever present economic demands.

E-Books

E-books are a product of the computer age and had their beginnings when institutions began putting copies of classics, which were not copyrighted on the Internet for personal consumption. The industry has grown to include many publications, with e-book editions of many standard works; its significance within the industry structure is at present minimal, but it cannot be ignored by the modern writer who is merchandising books.

The International Digital Publishing Forum in July 2007 reported that sales in the United States of e-books has quadrupled since 2002. The data was collected from 12-15 wholesalers who sell e-books. E-book copies of our books including *Writing as a Small Business,* are available on our publisher's website: www.outskirtspress.com. We are considering making them available on Amazon.com as well.

Amazon's "Search Inside the Book" program is similar to an e-book, but the method employed is cumbersome and takes time, so an author may wait six months or more for his title to appear in the program. If the book exists with the publisher in digital format, then there is no reason why the publisher can't transfer it to Amazon's program in an instant. The old, expensive, and outdated method of taking the book apart and scanning each individual page back to a digital file just clogs production.

Amazon wants to sell books, the publisher wants to sell books and authors want to sell books—the answer is staring them in the face. *Overhaul the system to interface with current*

Writing as a Small Business

technology. Stop trying to drive a Corvette with a buggy whip.

The world of e-books is an expanding avenue for you to explore while doing your market research.

Earlier we mentioned *"over production with emphasis on an obsolete format."* The hardbound title is the **dinosaur** of the industry, but it is still lumbering along, dragging its mystique. It will sink publishers except in specialized areas, the major one being editions for libraries, which must withstand heavy use from high circulation; the practice of stitching the folios to a cloth spur was replaced by glue ages ago. Another example are special editions of beautifully illustrated "coffee table" titles, such as art books and works of photographic studies, which are difficult to shelve in a library. They have a limited and specialized market.

Library jargon refers to hardbacks as "bound in boards." When a publisher asked Newberry award-winner Glen Rounds if he wanted his book, *Ole Paul, the Mighty Logger* bound in boards, Mr. Rounds replied, "Yes, that is an excellent idea." The original *Ole Paul*'s covers were real wood; now those first-run copies are exceedingly rare books.

A book inscribed by the author, which will only be read one time, has no reason to have a hardcover. Think in terms of taking up space, arthritic hands, cost of shipping, and weight lifting as good, sound economic reasons for change.

This is where the New York Times best-seller list misleads the beginning author as being the "holy grail" to which to aspire. The list is based on pre-ordered copies going to major chains, private bookstores, and libraries. If every library in the country ordered one copy for its collection, it would not make a significant difference in the numbers. Book clubs must wait a month or two after publication to take up a title. But these figures make up the best-seller lists.

Consumers then enter the picture. An author maybe on the best-seller list one week and be gone the next, because their productions are sitting on a display table collecting dust. A book has about 260 days after publication to make it before it is pulled from the shelves to make room for another.

Publishers pay fees to get their premier sellers on the front display tables as the customers enter the door. This is called "co-advertising." The same is true of the magazine displays around the checkout lanes at the grocery store.

The booksellers enjoy the privilege of not paying for their goods for a while and if volumes have not sold during a period of up to two years after publication, they can be returned to the publisher. Ingram, the largest book distributor in the country, has a return period of 180 days if it has a return agreement with the author.

What happens to these unsold copies? Supposedly, they are destroyed. We have a suspicion some may be sold in secondary markets (used books) or given as "obsolete merchandise" to charities as tax deductions for the publisher. Who eventually absorbs the cost of the unsold copies? The author—in reduced royalties, lower advances, or a dropped contract.

Some POD publishers, offer an insurance policy to their authors against returned titles. Others include this in the cost of their publishing packages. No matter how the process is handled, the author is the loser. A publisher cannot absorb the cost of titles that did not sell and still stay in business for very long.

One firm, NAIR, specializes in collecting obsolete merchandise from manufacturers for distribution to tax-exempt charities, senior citizen centers, schools, and libraries to be given away. Under the rules the merchandise cannot be resold by the recipient. Over the years, when I was a director of a public library, we would receive our NAIR order, for which the institution paid the shipping costs. Invariably, it would contain books from publishers. This is the reason I "suspect" not all copies are destroyed. My favorite item from this source is a heavy canvas bag with lots of pockets which fits over a five-gallon bucket. I've used it for years for my garden tools and it has yet to show any sign of wear.

Anatomy of a Bookstore.

This is a simple analysis of the costs of operating a bookstore in a small mall. The size and facilities have been kept tiny, but all of the factors—and more—are working in the background when a store owner agrees to carry your book.

> Ned Bookseller – Location: Stop in Mall Harrodsburg, KY – size 100 sq. ft.
> One employee – fixtures – inventory – fixed expenses

For Ned's example, we used the current cost of shelving, computer, cash register, table, a display shelf, checkout desk, seating, and workdesk from Gaylords's catalog (a company that supplies these items to libraries). We measured and counted the number of books on a standard shelf and used a unit cost/volume of ten dollars.

Ken Beard, CEO of Lakeland Insurance, Russell Springs, Kentucky, and Barbara Morgan, CEO of Morgan Real Estate, Lexington Kentucky, supplied the general figures and information used to calculate the monthly expenses for Ned Bookseller. We used a Kentucky town of Harrodsburg, which is outside of a major metropolitan area.

Writing as a Small Business

Ned's expenses for one month:

Rent @ 12.00/sq. ft.	$ 1200
Insurance on facilities & books	50
Utilities	
Electric, gas, water, Internet, Phone	1750
Advertising	
Media & Print	500
Office expenses & supplies	300
Salaries & Benefits for one employee includes Social Security, Workman's Comp. & Medicare @ 6.48/hour	1170
CAM (Common Area Maintenance) @7.50/hr 20 hours/week	605
Prorated cost of equipment for five years/mo.	2760
Prorated cost of inventory for one year/mo.	6770
Total operating expenses/mo.	$15105

Ned has an inventory of 8000 books for sale, a capital investment of $80,000 in merchandise. His profit margin per book is $2.50.

This means Ned Bookseller must sell 6,042 books (over half of his inventory), just to meet his current expenses for one month, before he can order new books or have any profit to purchase his own groceries.

Ned isn't compliant with the American Disabilities Act, which mandates enough space between the shelving for a wheelchair to make the turns around the shelves. Wider aisles means less floor space that can be devoted to shelving and display, but this is a factor for a real owner who has a business open to the public, along with many other federal, state, and local regulations that increase costs for the seller.

If Ned operated his store in a large metropolitan mall, his costs and the number of books he would need to sell each month would multiply exponentially. Cincinnati, Ohio, floor space is quoted to potential store operators for 30 dollars/square foot, which is still a long way from New York, Chicago, Miami, Los Angeles, or Seattle in terms of basic retail space.

Major bookstore chains will "anchor" a mall. They are the drawing card that brings people to the mall who, while there will shop other stores. A rental arrangement may be made with the owners of the mall for a set yearly lease fee of ten years or more. Over and above the lease agreement the bookstore proprietor will submit a quarterly profit-and-loss statement, and the owner will take another two to three percent of the profits as they occur. Within the lease agreement is a clause to the effect that the stores' books are open for examination at any time by the owners.

How does this information affect you as an author? You want to be one of those authors whose

Writing as a Small Business

books have enough selling power to earn Ned a profit over and above his expenses. What incentive can you offer Ned to carry your books?

Joe Konrath uses a public thank-you and personal visits. On the acknowledgment page of his novels, he includes the names of store owners who carry his books and the names of bookstore employees who hand sell a number of his books. He makes a point to remember the names of people who sell his books and often uses the name of a super salesman of his books for a character's name in one of his stories.

The next time you read or hear derogatory comments about booksellers consider this example. They are the unsung heros near the bottom of the "food chain" in the industry of publishing. If you want to have fun with higher mathematics, consider one of the major chains or large independents, whose facilities occupy 20,000 to 40,000 square feet, and run the cost of operation calculations.

Who is reading?

Where is your market and who is your audience? Below is a second string quote from another American Library Association newsletter:

> "The Reading Habits of Americans
> One in four adults say they have read **NO** books at all in the past year according to

an Associated Press–Ipsos poll released August 21. Of those who did read, women and seniors were the most avid, and religious works and popular fiction, were the top choices. Excluding those who hadn't read any, the usual number of books was seven. . . ."

Associated Press, August 21, 2007

These demographic figures have been fairly standard for years. Women and seniors read books. Women purchase most of the books. Is it any wonder that "chick lit" became a high roller? Marketing experts are aware of these figures. Part of a strong query letter to an agent is a well-conceived marketing plan. So where do you find your market, once your book is published? Who are your intended readers and where are they located?

Let's Talk about Money

Money in regards to authorship is an area largely ignored by publications for authors. A general attitude prevails that authors should be above mundane considerations like money. Writers should live solely for their craft because having the funds to pay the electric bill is outside one's creative endeavors. *Writer's Digest*, October 2007 has a number of articles and advice for author's about money, but they run to cutting personal costs,

Writing as a Small Business

finding ways to end being subsidized by a spouse, or reality situations about promotion of a book. It's like it has finally dawned on someone that writers are getting "short changed" in the economic department of their lives.

As authors we can't count the number of words that have been written about the evils of money. It is a favorite topic in many mysteries, but those words influence our attitudes about money, whether we are aware of it or not. The subject needs a good hard "reality check."

Money, in and of itself, is a medium of exchange for *ordinary and necessary* expenses. It is nothing more than a tool, much like a pencil. It is easier to carry around than stones. It is more honorable to use when dealing with fellow humans than a club.

The man who wrote the first dictionary, Samuel "Dr." Johnson said it this way:

> "No one, but a blockhead ever wrote except for money." April 5, 1776. *Familiar Quotations,* p. 432

We've also found that the best and most explicit defense of the right to copyright was written by John Milton in his *Aeopagitica* in 1644. These early titans of literature knew what they were talking about, and their observations have not been proven invalid during the subsequent years. You, as an author, should take their advice well in hand and follow the direction of Judge Learned Hand to arrange your affairs to ensure your taxes are as low as possible. Then follow the instructions of Joe Konrath and treat yourself like a business. The advantage is yours.

Who can help you get published?

Here, in-depth market research is advisable. Purchase a copy of *Guide to Literary Agents* for the current year. Like *Writer's Market*, it has some valuable information in the little essays and articles between the listings. The 2006 edition has an excellent article, "Know Your Rights," on pages 76-81. What rights does the traditional publisher and small press acquire when your book is sold? What rights are negotiable and what rights does the author retain? The circle graphs are enlightening and worth the cost of the volume. It is a keeper on our reference shelf.

Other places to investigate are *Publisher's Weekly,* agents appearing at workshops and conferences, the Web, or agents who write for *Writer's Digest*. Checking out the author's acknowledgments in the books you read is another source for names.

You may notice phrases in your research and endeavors: "no previous publications," "only consider referrals," "not accepting in this genre," or others of the same generalization; then, it is time to

Writing as a Small Business

investigate other avenues. After four years and pushing 70, we investigated print on demand. We still have the binder, the covers, paper cutter and spines from our first efforts, which may be dusted off for special publications such as a Brewster County cookbook.

When the rejection letters pile up with little explanation as to why, the entire world of self-publishing is open to you. Three books to read when considering self-publishing are: Brent Sampson's, *Publishing Gems* and *Self-Publishing Simplified,* plus Dan Poynter's *Self-Publishing Manual.* There are many others and a search on Amazon.com will locate them.

This chapter has been a brief overview of the industry from the standpoint of market research and it is by no means complete. How do you utilize the expenses you incurred while pursuing your market survey?

Chapter 5
Keeping Your Records

Our method of keeping records involves three simple tools: a small spiral-ring notebook, the spreadsheet program installed on our computer as part of the operating system, and an expandable file.

It does not matter if you are a perennial *New York Times* best-seller nominee or have just written your first word. Before the IRS, everyone is equal with the same rights and responsibilities.

**You declare income when it occurs.
You take an expense for the calendar year in which it occurs.**

Acquire a small notebook that will fit in a

shirt pocket, and don't leave your bedroom without it. They sell them at Wal-Mart in packs of three. This is the simplest method of keeping a travel/expense diary and is required in tax court, in some form, for documentation of your everyday expenses. This is where, as in your novel, the details and their accuracy are of major significance.

To make the IRS happy, each record and receipt should contain the following information:
Date—Provider—Cost—Purpose.

If your vehicle does not have an odometer that you can set for a single trip, write down the date and mileage after you turn the key. Then record the milage again when you pull back in your parking area. Simple subtraction will give you the total miles driven. After you have completed the math, draw a line under the answer or circle it.

When you make numerous trips to the same location, it is not necessary to make elaborate notes in your travel/expense notebook.

Example:
 10/4/07 – library: return reference materials – 20 miles.

This is a sufficient notation. Just make sure the recorded mileage to the same location in the spreadsheet is consistent throughout the document. If you are using multiple libraries, as we do, indicate the location.

You live in the city and use public transit.

Writing as a Small Business

Record the coins dropped in the box in the notebook, and do the same for taxi service or any other form of transportation for which you are not given a receipt.

What did you do while on your trip? No, going to the grocery does not count unless you picked up some paperclips, glue, or other supplies that are used for your business of writing. Mark them on your receipt, note the item and amount in your diary, enter it on your spreadsheet, and then place the receipt in your file.

This means always clean out your pockets before tossing your clothes in the laundry basket. The IRS frowns on globs of paper that have been through the washer and will disallow the deduction unless you go back and obtain a duplicate (the trip to correct your mistake is not deductible).

> Tax court is the U.S. Tax Court, but tax decisions can also be rendered by the U.S. District and Courts of Appeals, U.S. Federal Claims Court, and the U.S. Supreme Court. Each decision affects the Code and its administration. The courts may rule against the IRS and in favor of the taxpayer.

A notebook is the oldest, easiest, and simplest method of keeping records and it is mandatory in tax-court cases as evidence. There are plenty of firms willing to sell you a product for keeping records, but we have never found one that has not had problems. Size is a major consideration—if it is too big to fit in your pocket or purse, the first thing you know it will be residing on the dresser.

The notebook is also there to jot notes of a facial expression, a turn of a phrase you overhear in a restaurant, or a description of the slant of the sun on the clock above the courthouse. We are not in business to sell you a record-keeping system, but from this point on we will assume you own a computer.

Keep the notebooks to back up the computerized records, along with your paid receipts, no matter how many places you make duplicate copies of your computer files. Experience has taught us to use two auxiliary disks besides the desk top. We do not store tax information on our hard drive, those components "give up the ghost" when it is the least convenient.

What Records Do You Keep?

It almost comes under "If someone hands you a slip of paper **keep it.**" Keep all receipts for purchases used in your work, or to promote your work. Rejection letters have intrinsic value, so keep them and include other documentation that supports the items listed in your travel/expense diary.

Why do rejection letters have value? They provide supporting evidence that you are seeking to

Writing as a Small Business

make a profit from your endeavors, not using your hobby as a means of acquiring status as a sole proprietor.

> Cut-and-Paste with a bottle of glue. Our sales sheet for *Qualifying Laps* on our publisher's website does not fit on one page. The second page has one line: the name and address of the publisher. When submitting copies for review, the recipient hates getting more than one page. To solve the problem, I cut the address from a page and pasted it to the bottom of a blank sheet below the margin setting, made copies of the paste-up, and used those sheets to print out the sales sheet. The bottle of glue and the trip to the grocery were a necessary expense for *Qualifying Laps*.

Hobby expenses are not deductible under the Internal Revenue Code. There are a few instances where hobby expenses can be deducted under personal deductions on the standard 1040, but *only* to the extent of the income produced. *Self-Employed Tax Solutions* has a concise description of the difference between hobby and business expenses on pages 8-15.

When *Qualifying Laps* was published, we submitted it to 16 reviewing services, along with the other documentation necessary for this procedure. We also included a stamped, self-addressed postcard with two phrases: "___ may be considered" and "___ not at this time." All that was needed on the other end was a check mark in the appropriate blank and pitch it in the out going mail, with no commitment on the part of the recipient. Of those submissions, three postcards were returned, one with a note thanking us for thinking of them, but all were rejections.

The one from *Publisher's Weekly* was the fun one. It was not marked, nor was the postage canceled, but it arrived back in our mailbox. The other 13, we assume, went in the trash unopened.

The important thing is that those rejections are documented by the cost of the books, the cost of the mailers, and the receipt from the U.S. Postal Service listing all 16 submissions and their destinations which can be cross-referenced to the printed list of names and addresses, the travel/expense diary, and our spreadsheet file. This constitutes four separate support documents for our efforts to merchandise our book (not to entertain ourselves in our old age).

Create a Spreadsheet for Your Records.

Operating systems for computers contain a simple spreadsheet program. On the screen they resemble the old green bookkeeping-ledger sheets from an office supply store. Each program has different instructions and its own style, but basically they all function in the same fashion.

Writing as a Small Business

When you first open your program, give your spreadsheet file a name and with the year in the title. IF Publishing resides on our desktop and is saved periodically to two other disks with a check in the "make a backup box" marked. It is a Microsoft Works Spreadsheet 7.0 file.

Back it up at the moment you name the file. Very ugly things occur, no matter how careful you are. The stories of people who had all of their records on/in one source and lost them due to computer crashes, fire, flood etc. are legendary.

When your spreadsheet is saved, next create a word file. Your word file must explain and substantiate each column of your spreadsheet and the safeguards you have employed to maintain its integrity. *You must keep this word description of your system for as long as you use the system.* Each year, we make a copy of the word file and re-label it; when we make a change to the file, it is dated and the reason for the change is noted in the word file.

At the end of the accounting period, which is normally a calendar year, your entries will compose a written record of your business proceedings.

Store a paper copy of the completed spreadsheet and word file with your paper records and receipts. Note the method of freezing a spreadsheet in your word file. The procedure for Microsoft 7.0 is under "Format" in the toolbar. For IRS auditors, they must be in a form that cannot be tampered with or changed prior to the audit.

Extra precaution: At the close of your accounting year, save a **read-only** CD file of your records and organization procedure. Label it as to the year and place the CD in a safe deposit box. Protect your records in every manner that you can.

If you have access to a scanner, scan the receipts to the CD, or use a digital camera and load the pictures to the CD. Check to make sure they are legible before completing your operation. We live in an electronic world and events of recent years have taught us hard lessons that should not be ignored.

Data protection services were just coming into existence prior to my retirement when libraries began saving their massive data bases to an outside source. Over the years, I helped restore a number of libraries after vandalism, floods, and tornadoes. The physical labor alone took years, and we would have been very grateful to have had help from an outside source. If an electronic service had been available, we would have used it, as all of these endeavors were to help another librarian who was in trouble. Just this past month, I noticed in the American Library Association Bulletin that the process of restoring libraries is beginning in Louisiana and Mississippi.

I have mentioned our membership in AAA and was surprised to see this announcement in their Nov/Dec 2006 magazine. They are offering to their members a 10percent discount on their monthly bill for membership with **Argati**.

Writing as a Small Business

Argati offers an online data backup solution for the home or business at affordable prices. All of your files are copied to a remote center automatically. For more information on this disaster data recovery system see www.argati.com/AAA.

Chapter 6
Building Your Spreadsheet

There has been no attempt to create anything but a simple add-up-the-column spreadsheet record. It is very conservative creative accounting is a term in many minds, synonymous with fraud. You know how long it takes to develop the perfect plot or outline. The time and effort it takes to develop a spreadsheet or accounting system to hide fraud is not worth it. The IRS auditors are highly trained to see right through anything that amateurs can dream up.

List the income and expenses as they occur, and total the columns at the end of the year. There are several commercial programs designed to do tax accounting. Our advice is to wait until you become proficient in a simple system before moving to something more sophisticated. Even *Quicken*, the grand daddy of them all for home use, requires some degree of expertise.

It is easy to put off doing this mundane work that has nothing to do with your creative projects, but it is like committing suicide to let it pile up until you are overwhelmed. This, from a Chinese fortune cookie, explains it all:

"Delay is the deadliest form of denial."

Waiting to do it until the night before your appointment with your tax professional is sadomasochistic behavior. Develop a habit of entering your data and filing your receipts frequently; it is very easy to forget something important because you are dealing with details.

Jeffery Zbar expressed it this way in his article for *Writer's Digest,* "Of Football and Taxes," December 2002: Don't wait until the end of the game to start planning your defense for taxes. A good game plan begins before the beginning of the game; for taxes this is the first day of a calendar year or when you begin writing with the intent of publication.

Your Spreadsheet

You are working on a cash basis, which is accounting terminology. The term means you are working with income as it occurs and expenses when they are incurred.

Writing as a Small Business

The screen is divided into columns and rows separated by lines. A block inside the lines is "a cell." One very nice feature is found in the top tool bar under **FORMAT**. Open Format and scroll down to **ALIGNMENT**, open Alignment—under the Vertical settings box is a small box to click for wrap-around text. This must be set while you are working in an individual cell. It is invaluable when your item description exceeds the allotted number of spaces in the cell.

To the right of the spreadsheet are all the instructions for adjusting cells, columns, and rows, written in clear English. If you have never used a spreadsheet, spend some time getting familiar with the operations. Some very successful authors use them to create outlines and time lines for keeping their books on track. Free lancers use them as appointment schedules and as cost analysis for time spent on a project.

You must also set the format to print the **lines** for the columns and rows for a paper copy. They show on the screen but do not print unless you tell the computer to tell the printer to do so. Doing this makes your paper copy easier to read.

How wide you make each column depends on how many numerals your expense record requires. The spreadsheet we've created fits comfortably on a legal size paper printed "landscape" style. The first two columns are imperative.

Column A – Label it **Date** or put the year in place of the word "date"

If this is your first year as an author, begin your spreadsheet as

January 1 of the calendar year. Remember all the market research you did while producing your manuscript—this is a good place to include them in your expenses. At the beginning of your calendar year for your new business, with this spreadsheet these early research expenses will be posted to Column T.

When the expense occurred: The date should correspond with the date on your receipt/check and in your notebook. There is no reason to record check numbers in your travel/expense notebook because your check register and bank statement serve the same purpose.

In an effort the save spaces, put the year at the top of this column; then you only need to list the month and day down the column.

Example: Column A, 2008, below in row is the date 1-2, (Jan. 2).

Our system includes the full year automatically if we use the slash "/" between the numerals, which takes up unnecessary spaces.

Column B – Label it **Item**

What is the expense? This is where the wrap-text feature of the spreadsheet allows you to be more specific. Make sure you set it while you are in the particular cell you want to expand.

Enter the name of the firm, restaurant, bookstore, post office with location, etc. Your travel/expense day diary is where you record the purpose for the item and on the receipt itself. This is a case of being brief but explicit.

Column C – Label it **Check Number**

Ours reads "C#" to save spaces. Industry experts tell me paper checks are on their way out. We no longer get checks returned, but we have the bank statement, paid receipt, and check register as proof of purchase. **Canceled checks or credit card statements are not acceptable as proof of purchase by the IRS.** The paid receipt is the major supporting evidence of a tax-deductible item. It must include this information: **date, amount, item or service rendered**. From force of habit we note date, payment amount and check number on every bill paid.

We are considering dropping this column, as the check number is recorded on the paid receipt and serves no purpose with the IRS. Old habits die hard, but it is one less item to fool with. If you decide to go this route, remember to note the check number on the paid receipt because going back through the checkbook or your bank statement takes time.

At times when you must pay with cash for an item, write yourself a receipt. We shop for used books at flea markets, which operate on a cash basis. They are one of the best places to locate reference books, like a bartender's guide or a medical encyclopedia at a low cost.

"A," "B," and "C" columns will not be added at the end of the accounting period or end of the calendar year. The following will be the column designations that compose your year-end calculations, with an explanation of the kinds of expenses, which are included in each individual column.

Column D – Label it **Mileage**
Enter the information from your notebook frequently. Do not try to calculate the monetary value. Escalating gasoline costs precipitated two IRS costs/mile for the taxable year of 2005. Previously, the figure set in January was valid for the entire year, as it was for the tax year **2006**. Take your spreadsheet to your tax preparer with each trip dated; he/she will have the necessary allowances. The information is also posted to the IRS website, www.irs.gov/.

Writing as a Small Business

Column E – Label it **Direct Sales**

These are the sales you make yourself or sell on consignment. This may be the most important column of your spreadsheet. It is possible to manage for two years as you experience "start up costs," without showing an income from your business, but after this period you should have some income. The general rule is three out of five *consecutive* years. Note that here we've referred to income, which is different from profit. It is not mandatory that you have an income from a small business during the early years, but *it cannot go on forever*. Income and profit are not the same thing.

Your documentation is of the greatest importance. What you have to prove to an IRS auditor is your *intent* to sell your articles or books. For four years, prior to 2004 we sent out query letters trying to secure an agent to no avail. Our copies of the *2003 and 2006 Guide to Literary Agents* are dog-eared, under-lined and dated as to when a letter was mailed. These books have become part of our supporting documentation for our efforts to conduct our writing efforts as a small business.

> For Nash Black it was the middle year after IF Publishing was reactivated. In two years, 2003 and '04, he sold some pieces, but for 2005 he couldn't peddle "copy about a mouse convention to a cat." 2006 was a better year, with the publication of *Qualifying Laps*. He had direct cash sales but has yet to receive a royalty check. For 2007 direct sales, gratuities, sales through online booksellers and bookstores established Nash Black as an author when *Tax, Stumbling Blocks and Pitfalls for Author 2007, Sins of the Fathers,* and *Travelers* were published.

Finally, as the calendar kept creeping forward for us, we reached the decision that if we didn't want to be published posthumously we would investigate publishing through print on demand, which was a mere infant in the world of publishing when we began our search for an agent and publisher.

Direct sales, grants, stipends, gratuities, sale-of-rights, advances, and royalties are all income for authors and all except *direct sales* are handled on forms other than the Schedule C. We will explain each and give our reason for positioning it on the spreadsheet but will follow the lines on the Schedule C as closely as possible. Remember, in some instances you are fitting a square peg in a round hole, and it must fit exact.

Writing as a Small Business

Columns "**A—Date**" "**B—Item,**" "**C—Check Number,**" "**D—Milage,**" and "**E—Direct Sales**" are standard entries for a business spreadsheet. If you do not pay expenses by check, there is no reason to include the column; simply adjust the labels to fit your needs.

Then continue across the row through the alphabet with your labels getting them as close as possible to the lines on the IRS Schedule C Profit or Loss From Business (Sole Proprietorship) – OMB No.1545-0074 form. Some expenses are covered on the back of Schedule C, Part III – Cost of Goods Sold and Part V – Other Expenses.

We have ignored lines and one entire section on the Schedule C that do not pertain to authors or artists. The forms were designed for businesses with receipts in the millions of dollars and employees. Your expenses will be in the hundreds or low thousands with no employees, except contract labor if you employ someone to do your typing, research, or editing.

Now your spreadsheet is set up and saved; each time you add an entry be very careful to locate the correct cell of the proper row and column. As you proceed, it will be beneficial to print out a copy of the first page with the column designations. This makes it easier to locate the correct cell for your entry, because the entire sheet will not show on the screen. Keep it near your computer, as this saves you from scrolling to the top of the spreadsheet each time to make sure you are in the correct position. Review the entries periodically for errors and omissions; they are as easy to make as a misplaced comma.

In one respect, keeping records requires rethinking everything you do and every action you take in light of your business activities. Doing so makes a difference; it did for us. We were missing items the first few years because we were thinking as authors, not business people. Even today, the mind will click into gear, and we will realize that an activity and the milage is a business expense, because we had never stopped to consider it in that light.

State Sales Taxes

This is general information, but it is one of the most frequently asked questions by new authors doing direct sales. We can tell you how the state sales tax operates in Kentucky but not in other states.

Writing as a Small Business

> Nash Black had a booth in an antique mall in another state. He acquired a retail sales permit that was never used to purchase items for resale just for utilization when paying the retail sales tax on sales made within that state. Later he pulled out of the mall and ceased operation within the state. Several years passed. Then he received a bill for sales tax on estimated sales that were never made, **for a period when he was not doing business in the state**. It took two years and many phone calls and letters from a lawyer to clear the mistake from the state's computer system. His error was in not having canceled the retail-sales permit. **Remember this if you move your residence to another state. Neglect is costly.**

Make plans, seek information, and acquire a retail sales license before you sell your first book to your neighbor across the street. Do not put this action off, or you may be charged a whopping sum from your state revenue department for *their estimate* of your sales.

See Appendix II. We have obtained the sales-tax permit registration information from all 50 states and the District of Columbia for your benefit. Our age is showing because many states handle this online—locating an old-fashioned mailing address was a problem.

The amount of the sales tax shown for each state

was taken from *The World Almanac for 2007*, pp. 557-585, along with each states' Web address. It was correct when the information was submitted to that publication, but it is subject to change with a meeting of state legislatures. At this writing, Alaska, Delaware, Montana, New Hampshire, and Oregon do not have a sales tax. This is an area where the Internet has major problems when trying to locate an individual state's department of revenue. Homeland Security has created some very strange situations.

Most states have their own method of collecting a sales tax on direct sales of merchandise made within that state by their residents. Contact the department of revenue for your state (located in the state capital) and acquire a retail-sales license. Call your local public library; it generally has a state directory of offices and phone numbers in the reference section.

Mention, **if you are given a chance**, that you are an author and would prefer to file annually instead of quarterly. It costs more to process your small check (under $40) than the amount of the check. When you sell a book within the boundaries of your state of residence and it has a sales tax, you must pay a retail-sales tax. How you collect the tax is up to you.

We have had a Kentucky retail-sales license for a long time, as we have other business entities. For our first book, when we sold *Qualifying Laps* at a signing at the public library or a book fair, we

Writing as a Small Business

priced the volume at $15.00 and absorbed the tax. This means that our book actually sold for $14.10, as Kentucky has a 6% sales tax. The price was fair, with a good discount below shelf price; it also helped making change easier when we were concentrating on writing inscriptions. We kept a stash of five-dollar bills just for the purpose of making change, as most people handed us a twenty in payment.

When we sell outside our state or ship books by mail to an address in another state, the sales are not taxable under current Kentucky laws. We have noticed in various publications that this may change. There have been proposals before Congress in recent months to institute a nationwide "use" tax to counteract the impact on state revenues of online purchasing where the state sales tax does not apply. A use tax is as the name implies: the consumer pays a tax for the use of the product. Remember the Stamp Act prior the American Revolution? It is the same principle.

When we have a signing at a bookstore and the owner supplies the volumes, it is his responsibility to collect the sales tax, because it is his merchandise being sold. We also have copies of our books at a local bookstore on consignment; the owner collects the sales tax and declares it on his monthly tax statement. This service alone is worth the 20 percent we pay him for carrying our products.

Column F – Label it **Sales Tax Collected**

For accounting purposes; we pay the sales taxes collected the previous year in January. This means that for the year in which it was collected it was "income" and will not become an expense until the calendar year in which it actually is paid to the Kentucky Department of Revenue. In our case, books sold and the tax collected in 2006 are both income, as this was our first year to sell books under the reactivated IF Publishing. The tax collected in 2006 was not an expense until 2007.

Posting your accounting of the sales tax collected beside the entries for your direct sales makes it easier to understand which sales were taxable and which were non-taxable for your state's sales-tax report. For the Kentucky sales-tax return we must report both the taxable and non-taxable sales.

Column G – Label it **Advances & Royalties**

Advances and royalties are reported separately from direct sales on Schedule E **(not Schedule C),** but locating your income from this source at the beginning of the spreadsheet makes for continuity.

Writing as a Small Business

> Example: Nash Black is awarded a grant for $3500 from the Kentucky Humanities Council to finish a book on taxes—a little help with the utilities and groceries while he is working on his project. The Council owns no rights to the finished product. Hence, the grant is income to be reported.

Report all non-direct sales income on Schedule E.

The important thing is that the income must not be ignored because the grantor of grant is obligated under their "operations charter" to file a 1099-MISC with the Internal Revenue Service under your name and social security number if the amount paid in grants, gratuities, and stipends in any calendar year is over $600. For many organizations which operate under 401C-3, tax-exempt laws will automatically file a 1099-MISC for each disbursement no matter what the sum or style of the remuneration.

Column H – Label it **Review Copies**
When you submit a copy of your book to *Publishers Weekly* indicate it in this column with a one (1). We submitted 16 copies of *Qualifying Laps* for review, so the numeral 16 would be in this cell on the same row as the postage expense. The cost of these books

to you is calculated at the end of the year using MERCHANDISE PURCHASED, so at this point you only need the total number of books, not the cost of an individual book.

Begin Your Expenses Columns

Make these columns correspond as closely as possible with the expense-item lines listed for Part II of the Schedule C form. Accountants and auditors do not think in the same terms you do, so follow their examples for your expenses and record the procedures in your word file. We are using the designation of expenses used by our tax professional when filling out our return.

For large one-time expenses, we make a note in the rows below the normal entries on the spreadsheet. Some of these are equipment purchases, yearly mortgage interest, home-owners insurance, property taxes, repair and maintenance to our home, etc.

This method eliminates the need for columns with only one entry and saves time when using your spreadsheet for calculations. For lack of a better word we call them "FOOTNOTES." Depending on your circumstances, there are several ways to utilize these expenses. A frank discussion with your tax professional should result in the procedure most beneficial to you; the expenses incurred by authors not only are different, but also each individual

Writing as a Small Business

situation is different.

A candidate for IF Publishing's "Footnotes" is the number and cost of the unsold copies on hand of *Taxes, Stumbling Blocks and Pitfalls for Authors 2007*, when we decided to republish under the new title, *Writing as a Small Business*. The unsold copies represent a business loss to IF Publishing within the category of "Obsolete Merchandise." "Stolen Merchandise" is also a business loss; we have had four books stolen from places where they are handled on a consignment basis. The information of this caliber should be entered into your notes for consideration in Section V—Other Expenses of Schedule C.

Below the "Footnotes" on the spreadsheet, we have another section for plain NOTES. An example of this: We have books out on consignment. We make a note of the number and when a volume is sold, we either restock or reduce the amount in our notes. This puts all of our marketing information in one single place and aids year-end calculations for the amount of inventory on hand.

The information about our home as to square footage, amount used for business, calculation of the value of the home minus the cost of the land is a permanent notation in our notes.

Column I – Label it **Advertising**

Expenses you employ to advertise your name as an author and your product are entered in this column. Examples are, business cards, costs of query letters, mass mailings, postcards, small donations with the expectation of making a sale, media advertising, business gifts, T-shirts with your book cover silk screened on the back, in other words, anything you do in the way of advertising and promotion of your book.

Business gifts for a sole proprietorship are limited at this writing to $25/individual gift within a calendar year and they must be given with the expectation of receiving a business consideration. A perfect business gift within the guide lines is *Writing as a Small Business*.

When you give a copy of your book to family members or friends tell them you would appreciate their writing a review on Amazon.com for your book. We were very proud of our first book and gave out copies in this fashion, but the reviews were not forthcoming. Instead of telling their friends about our book, which would have generated sales, our friends and family passed the book around. We learned our lesson and are not so generous at this point in our career. A business gift is one that is expected by the giver to generate sales or other monetary considerations. It isn't being stingy; *it's being business savvy.*

Column J – Label it **Commissions**
Payments you extend to others for

Writing as a Small Business

selling your work. If you leave copies of your book in a bookstore or a library for sale on consignment, the fee or percentage of purchase price you pay for this service is a commission. The restaurant where our book club meets has copies of our books for sale. This method of distribution has been very successful, especially on the night we meet, when other diners want to know who is in the backroom making all the noise.

Column K – Label it **Interest**

The interest on a designated (used **only** for your business) credit card is deductible. Use it for your writing expenses. If you should take out a loan against your home to set up your office and pay publishing costs, the interest for this loan is a business expense.

Obtain a credit card and **dedicate** it to your writing career. *Nothing* goes on the card except legitimate business expenses.

Monthly interest on a dedicated business card is an allowable deduction with the IRS, but not on other personal credit cards. *Under no circumstances use it for anything else.* The credit card statement gives you a paper record to cross-match against your receipts, spreadsheet, and travel/expense journal, but it does not, in and of itself, constitute proof of the expenditure.

Column L – Label it **Legal and Professional Services**

Expenses incurred when filing your taxes, the services of a lawyer, fees paid to your agent, etc., belong in this column.

Professional organizations that help to sell or promote your book: Sisters in Crime and Mystery Writers of America are examples.

We are members of the AAA (American Automobile Association) and have been since 1964. This is a business expense because each time we take a business trip, we get a "trip ticket" with maps to each of our destinations: libraries, hotels, bookstores, etc.

> A late-night drive across Illinois, Michigan, and Wisconsin without finding a motel vacancy taught us to use AAA's reservation service. Sleeping in a small hatchback at a rest stop on I-90 is not a restful experience prior to attending a business meeting.

We also arrange our overnight reservations through AAA, which is the same as using a travel agent and comes with the price of your membership. AAA has the facilities to make air trip reservations for you at the lowest available rates. Hotel and motels that display the AAA symbol will allow a

Writing as a Small Business

10% discount on your room no matter what your age.

One time we were checking in to a Hampton Inn, and we asked for the AARP (American Association of Retired Persons) discount and handed the clerk our AAA credit card. He looked at it and said, "I can't give you both discounts."

The trip ticket is documentation that we were on a business trip, not on a vacation, and it is filed with our receipts. Last year we attended a writing conference in Smyrna, GA. By accident, we learned of another service from reservations by AAA. It is not your address that is on the reservation but the address of the office of the AAA chapter that made the reservation for you—a valuable fringe benefit in this age of identity theft.

Column M – Label it **Office Expenses**

These are expenses you acquire in operating your business and office.

For a beginning author a major item is postage and shipping as you submit materials to agents or publishers; the manuscript boxes and mailers to submit copies for advertising and review.

Small repairs to equipment (under $50), small equipment such as a high-pixel digital camera and photo printer under $400, comfortable chair, desk, filing cabinets, book shelving, etc., are expenses you would not have otherwise. If you purchase them together then list them separately on your spreadsheet so as not to exceed your ceiling for one item. You set your own limits, within reason, for repairs and equipment, but expenses for larger items and repairs are reported on Form 4562 – Deprecation and Amortization, which is a supplement to the Schedule C.

Remember to make notes of your limits of the amount ceiling in your word file outline. This can be changed if economic conditions warrant the action. Put any major expense, like a new computer in your Footnotes. Keep it simple; a beginner can get bogged down and give up, but to do so is not profitable.

Column N – Label it **Supplies**

This column should be used to list expenses for items used in the operation of your business and office: paper, ink cartridges for the printer, pens, small notebooks, bottle of glue, the smart cards for the camera, a computer program for your website, disks for saving data, etc. TurboTax would be a supply because it is only valid for a single tax year.

Should you become confused with what goes in Office Expenses or Office Supplies, remember the *prepositions*. If it is used "to" operate the business, the item goes in Office Expenses. If it is used "in" the operation of

Writing as a Small Business

the business, it goes in Supplies—think in terms of expendable tools like mailers, paper, and pencils.

Column O – Label it **Taxes & Licenses**

When you pay your state's "sales tax collected," it goes in this column.

The cost of any licenses you may be required to purchase by your state in order to conduct direct sales goes in the same column. A few states require a deposit against paid sales taxes before you can obtain a permit to collect sales tax.

We live in a rural area, so a city permit to operate a business from home is not a problem. But in urban areas, licenses must be obtained and there is a fee attached. The fee would be an expense in this area. Many municipalities charge a fee for a permit to hold a garage sale. If you sell a few copies of your book, this is a tax expense item for your business.

Assessments added to your property tax bill for **maintenance** of sidewalks, streets, or sewers are deductible. An assessment to construct them is not deductible.

Self-Employment Taxes

Self-employment taxes **are not added** into this

column because your business does not pay the tax; **it is paid by an individual**. They are filed on Schedule SE. This information is a candidate for the footnotes at the bottom of your spreadsheet, as the amount owed cannot be calculated until all of your income and deductions are figured to produce your net earnings. *The payment will be made when net earnings information is available; hence, like the state sales tax, it is paid in the next calendar year and becomes an individual expense on the 1040 for the calendar year in which it is paid.* See Appendix I.

Column P – Label it **Travel & Lodgings**

We do not travel by air, but if you do, the cost of your plane ticket would go in this column. These are very carefully scrutinized in an audit and must be labeled with date, costs, destination, purpose, etc. Keep your boarding passes; most of the required information is printed on them. If you are traveling to a workshop, keep the program in your file with the sessions you attended marked as an additional supporting document.

Walker's *Self-Employed Tax Solutions* recommends keeping a travel diary with notations for sessions attended, contacts made, and other essential business-related memorandums. We have never done this, but we can see the value, especially when an author returns home and is trying to

Writing as a Small Business

remember the name of someone who could be important to his or her career. Obtain business cards and staple them on the page with your notes; then the vital information will not be lost.

Traveling with your spouse or companion? The question to answer is: *Is the presence of a second person necessary for the business?* We travel by land routes; one member of our team is blind in the left eye, which makes driving on an interstate highway difficult and might cause an accident, so we need to have a second person. There can be other reasons—besides consuming an alcoholic beverage—for using a designated driver.

When attending workshops, we split up and participate in different sessions, taking a tape recorder so we can share the information. We also register for the event as two separate participants under our own names.

Previously we mentioned AAA's reservation service. By using this, your room will be ready and waiting for you, and you have a complete record of the expense on the motel bill without employing a travel agent. Always request late check-in so you do not lose your reservation and be charged for it.

Big note: While rewriting *Taxes, Stumbling*

Blocks and Pitfalls for Author 2007, we discovered we had been cheating ourselves for years in regards to the next column, Column Q – Meals and Entertainment. A meal is a meal, right?

No, the IRS looks at meals differently.

The rule is: If you must stay away from your "tax home" overnight your meals are 100% deductible as a travel expenses, on line 24 a of Schedule C.

Up until this year we had never taken a meal deduction that was not incurred on a business trip. This alone is one of the reasons for a new book; the previous information was invalid.

Column Q – Label it **Meals & Entertainment**

This column is for business meals for interviews, thank-yous, research, etc. They occur during the course of an ordinary business day. They are deductible under the 50% rule (only one-half of the expense is allowed as a deduction). In other words, the business expense is for your guest, not you. Enter the full amount of the total bill for all parties in your expense column for meals.

Your agent or publisher should take you to lunch. But as an author, an efficient way to encourage a profitable interview is a relaxed lunch or dinner.

Record the purpose of the interview in your travel/expense notebook and on the receipt. Use a tape recorder and keep a copy of the tape in your files as proof of the purpose of the interview and expense. This procedure may make the person with whom you are conducting the interview uncomfortable—ask first. The tape recording is invaluable to you because you don't have to take notes.

Thank-you meals: Who feeds your cats, gets the mail, waters your plants and looks after your place when you are on a business trip?

In our case, it is my sister who lives next door. It doesn't matter that she is my sister; she is performing a service for us and deserves a thank-you. This is why we suggest putting the relationship on the receipt, being up front saves headaches. This expense is considered a gift by the IRS; as such, the deduction can only be for $25/individual/year. My sister rates trips to McDonald's, as the IRS has not purchased meals for years. The limit of $25/individual/year has been in effect for over a quarter of a century and not likely to change.

If we want to pump her for her medical knowledge, even as to how to spell medical terms, it is an interview and comes under the 50% rule. This is still less expensive than purchasing a medical encyclopedia, even at a flea market.

An excellent idea for documenting a business meal is found on p. 52 of *Self-Employed Tax Solutions.* Staple their business card to your restaurant receipt and write your purpose and your relationship on the recipient. An interview with Blaze Foto about his life as a book cover model for a vocational background as a career possibility for a novel is a business meal.

At this point we have reached the end of Part II on the Schedule C, except for line 25; this line is for the utilities in a separate establishment away from your home, which is more likely to apply to an artist than an author. For an author this expense is best entered on another form. Your cost of utilities will be utilized later on **Form 8892 – Expenses for Business Use of Your Home**, which is a sub-form of the Schedule C. Three more columns remain on our spreadsheet for consideration on Schedule C; the back side.

We give two copies of each of our publications to the library: one for the main library and one branch.

These copies put our name in the public eye. We have more than doubled our investment from the number of people who requested their own copy after reading the library's.

This is a business expense, which generated advertising, a book signing and book sales.

Column Q – Label it **Merchandise Purchased**
Column Q has two functions for your year end calculations.

Writing as a Small Business

Part I. First, look back to Column H, the number of volumes you have used as gifts and advertising. When you have totaled Column Q, the total gives you the complete cost of the books you've purchased for resale. Keep track of the total number of books purchased by entering the amount after the publisher's name in Column B – Item.

Example: Outskirts Press - 50v.

To obtain the total cost of gift, review and advertising copies of your books divide the total number purchased into the total cost of purchases. This gives you the unit cost of an individual title. Then multiply by how many have been used for business. This figure is then entered under Column I for advertising. To keep things simple, this should be your last entry for the year.

Doing this at the end of the year is easier than trying to keep track of the cost of each individual book. It is an average cost; you may purchase books under a special—no shipping costs. Different titles may have different wholesale costs. An average cost per volume is acceptable.

Part II. Your inventory for your direct sales.

These are copies of your books that you have purchased for resale at events not furnished by the publisher or a bookstore owner. Enter all of your direct purchases from the publisher. Private printings requires you to purchase the complete run of the volumes you ordered, while POD publishing enables you to purchase in various quantities to fulfill your needs.

We have no idea how this is handled by a traditional publisher for volumes you sell yourself. We will assume you do know. If you don't, then ask. It should be covered in your contract because books will not be given to you, and (this is an estimate) all authors—except the very top 3%—are involved in direct selling in some fashion.

At this point we are switching to Schedule C itself to explain a confusing accounting term for Part III – *Cost of Goods Sold*, which uses the information from Merchandise Purchased in two ways.

Schedule C — Part III Cost of Goods Sold. Located at the top on the back of the form.

Line 33 – Method Used – check the "a" box – **COST**

Line 34 – check **NO**

Line 35 – Inventory at the beginning

Writing as a Small Business

of the year.

If you have been doing this for a while, your beginning inventory is your ending inventory from the previous year. If you have no previous inventory, go to Line 36.

Line 36 – Purchases less cost of items withdrawn for personal use.

Divide the number of books purchased into the total of your purchases. **This will give you the cost of an individual book.**

Remember, you can only take an expense one time. Take the total cost of the books used for advertising and review, and subtract it from your purchases for the year. Enter the answer on **Line 36.**

Line 40 – Add lines 35 through 39.

Line 41 – Inventory at the end of the year.

Count the number of books you have on hand at the end of the year, and multiply that number by the average cost per volume.

Enter this figure on **Line 41.**

Line 42 – Cost of Goods Sold.

Subtract line 41 from line 40. Enter the result here and on page 1, line 4 of Schedule C.

The "cost of goods" sold is then subtracted from your gross sales on the front of Schedule C—Line 4 to give the gross profit or loss of your business, from which your deductions are taken or added to, to obtain your net profit or net operating loss (NOL).

Skip Section IV for **Information on Your Vehicle.** *Leave it blank.* This is an area difficult to prove, even if you've put signs all over the vehicle. You are taking your milage, which is much more beneficial to an author and you cannot take both. Our worst audit experience was over this question on the farm schedule and a pickup truck, years before trucks became the "in" transportation.

> At 12 degrees below zero, most of our records were frozen in the trunk of the car. The auditor asked, "What do you use a pickup truck for on a farm?" All I could see, in my mind, was carrying each bale of hay from the field to the barn. My brilliant answer; "To get from place to place." I immediately packed up what I had, walked out, and requested another auditor.
>
> Later, a friend who owned the largest dairy operation in the county and knew of my experience got the same guy, who asked the same question. Sam's answer, "To haul manure. Want a lift?"

Writing as a Small Business

Schedule C – Part V – Other Expenses

These are the unique item expenses for your small business as an author.

Given that there are about 150,000 books published per year in the United States, these are not items that concern the majority of small businesses—of which there are estimated to be 45 million who file Schedule C forms. The calculator says authors are 3 millionths of one percent of the filers who could file as a small business. Our tiny percentage of tax payers have expenses that are not part of the norm, Part V is the section that allows for these exceptions.

We have worked to reduce the number of items for inclusion in section V of the Schedule C. We state our reasoning in the word file of procedures followed for the spreadsheet. Technically, publishing expenses fall into Office Expenses as they are used "to" operate the business, but for clarity we list them in Part V – Other Expenses of the Schedule C.

Column S – Label it **Publishing Expenses**

These are the expenses incurred when you pay an agent or a publisher to publish and print your books. Agents charge for the costs of making multiply copies of your manuscript for their submission to various publishers. This is an expense, to you over and above their commissions. Commissions to agents are recorded in Column J, but usually it is deducted prior to any disbursements to you and is not a concern for your business accounting.

For those who utilize the services of a private press or print-on-demand service, the cost of each transaction should be recorded in Column S.

Column T – Label it **Editing and Research Materials.**

The payments you have made to an editor or reviewing service to prepare your manuscript for publication are recorded in this column.

We do not own a copier, so we get our necessary copies made at the public library. The cost of its service is entered here.

The cost of your Internet service could be included in the column if you do most of your research by this medium. If you go this route, you must keep a research log to indicate your usage, amount of time spent on this activity and the purpose of each search. Then the cost must be pro-rated between business and personal usage. We don't recommend it. Take the cost of Internet service under utilities on Form 8829 - Business Use of Your Home. There, you are taking a percentage anyway and do not need to keep usage logs or pro-rate an

Writing as a Small Business

expense that is now a normal way of operating a business.

Now, if you hire someone to search the Internet for "methods used in the domestication of monkeys," this would be a full business expense under research.

Research materials—you are an author, but you must read.

You can't obtain all the books you need from the library, and even inter-library loan has its limits. **You must begin building a professional library of your own**. Start with a good dictionary and thesaurus, the *Webster's New World*, editions in paperback are discounted for $3.87 at Wal-Mart. An example of the joys of electronic printing that are a good start for your writing career.

The public library frowns on underlining and highlighting its books. For us to write a book like this one, purchasing other books on taxes was a necessity. When we write about a rule or procedure, we want to be able to cite the reference for the said action. Then you can double-check us when necessary and will know where to look. All of the books we surveyed or read are listed in the bibliography. Put the cost of books you purchased in this column.

Your early market research expenses are recorded in this column.

We have two Listamainas on Amazon.com: *Books for Authors on Taxes and Tax Planning* and

Tax Help for Authors as a Small Business. These lists recommend books on taxes we used for *Writing as a Small Business*. If we have read the book, we will tell you in the notes, and the list will be updated as publications change. We, also, post individual reviews to Amazon for the titles we have read.

The website www.pennhand.com is devoted to reviews of mysteries and books on financial planning, taxes, and other publishing considerations. In this manner the tax manuals we purchased have been utilized five times as both resources and in the promotion of our book. They are a legitimate business deduction.

Column U – Label it **Utilities**

The cost of your utilities—electric service, water and sewerage, gas, garbage collection, phone, Internet service etc.—is entered in this column but is not utilized on Schedule C. We mentioned that we live in a rural area; we belong to a non-profit homeowners association, in which 98% of the dues we pay are used for street lights from RECC. Our dues are entered under utilities. These expenses are used on **Form 8829 – Expenses for Business Use of Your Home**.

We must divide ours between two separate businesses: IF Publishing and Years Ago. They occupy different areas of our home.

Writing as a Small Business

Supplements to Schedule C

It is difficult to exist and write without a roof over your head. Block out an area of your home, and do your best to designate this space as your business space—a space where the tools of your trade reside. Ideally, you can work in that space undisturbed. We have no idea where that silly ideal originated. Maybe from the same engineer who designed the new by pass around our county seat and expected tractor trucks dragging fifty-four-foot trailers to execute a 45-degree-angle turn to enter the new freeway.

Form 8829 – Expenses for Business Use of Your Home

Use a tape-rule; measure both the length and width of your home and your office space. Then multiply the length by the width for the total square footage of each area. If you have your house plans, the total square footage is listed in the bottom right-hand corner. Divide the square footage of the office area by the square footage of your home. The little number divided by the big number will give you a percentage. This figure is used to calculate the expense ratio of your office.

Form 8829 has lines for either rent or mortgage interest; other items are real estate taxes, insurance, utilities, repairs and maintenance, casualty losses, and depreciation (part III). Some of this information will be included in your footnotes, even if you or your mortgage escrow account is billed semi-annually or quarterly. Our mortgage is paid in full, so the bills for property taxes and insurance come directly to us.

A note of warning about **not depreciating** your home. A condo would qualify but an apartment that you rent will not, because you do not have a deed to the property. We do not intend to leave our home until we go feet first, but we are retired and settled in one place.

The tax professionals we interviewed advise their clients to take a deduction if they are entitled to it and can provide supporting documents to substantiate the claim. The Internal Revenue Service is not going to send you a letter saying, "You were entitled to this deduction, and we amended your return."

You must take this deduction because the complex wording in the IRC has implied to the courts that even if you did not take it but were *eligible* to take it will be considered as income on a home sale.

When you sell a home that has been used for business and depreciated you must recapture **all deprecation taken or were eligible to take on previous tax returns, beginning May 6, 1997**.

Said deprecation must be declared as income, even though the exclusion for capital gain on the home covers your capital gain if you have met all

Writing as a Small Business

the stipulations to qualify for the exclusion.

Schedule D– **Capital Gains & Losses Sale of a Home Used for Business**.

This is a very complicated IRS procedure, so discuss it with your accountant and your realtor who are both knowledgeable in this area; just be aware that it does exist in the current IRC. This is another area where a 1099-MISC is filed with the IRS from the real estate company that handled the sale of the home.

Form 4562 – **Depreciation and Amortization**

Depreciation and amortization are used to depreciate a large purchase (your computer) over its expected lifetime. The standard life of a computer is three to five years, but we are conservative, and depreciate the purchase price over a ten-year period. This form is where your footnotes are valuable.

Schedule E – The four types of authorship incomes are lumped together under royalties on this form. Expenses can be taken on a Schedule E but remember, a single expense item can be taken only one time. Your tax preparer will know where to take an expense to give you the best advantage.

Advances, grants, gratuities, royalties, and stipends where a 1099-MISC may or may not be issued in your name, and social security number to the Internal Revenue Service are income for Schedule E. You should—but may not—receive a copy of the 1099 filed in your name.

These items are not considered earned income by the IRS. Hence, if you are in the 62+ but not yet 65+ age bracket of Social Security, where your outside earnings are limited before restitution must be made to the Social Security System, these earning are not a concern. The Social Security limit is not affected by income from interest, dividends, or royalties, as they are not considered "earned income" by the IRS. Under the term "royalties," the IRS is primally interested in the income generated from gas, coal, and oil leases, not the income generated by the sale of books, but they are dumped in the same bucket.

Advances that are not loans: These constitute an interesting case, in that, in one sense, all advances are loans against royalties. You will not receive a royalty check from a traditional publisher until the advance has been covered in full.

Karen Robards, a New York Times best-selling Kentucky author spoke at a workshop we attended. She has had 26 books published and just now is beginning to get royalty checks.

Writing as a Small Business

These checks are for paperback editions of her early career books. It is a long road, even for someone who has national name recognition. Her major earnings come from advances.

Advances are generally paid in three parts: at the signing of the contract, the delivery of the manuscript, and acceptance of the manuscript. This gives an author a chance to do a little financial planning by managing for the payments to be paid in two calendar years.

Grants from foundations: These include grants from non-taxable institutions where the grantor has no financial interest in your publication project. They are not the same as the non-taxable student grants.

Gratuities for speaking engagements: A small sum may be given to you as an author to cover expenses, etc., by the group that invites you to speak. If you sell books at the same engagement, you will have three entries on the row of your spreadsheet in different columns if it is within your state.

Please do not expect this if you are invited to speak. For the most part it is not within the means of an organization to provide remuneration. The chance to sell your books is the advantage.

Authors are hitting book clubs hard, so

there is a lot of competition for a speaking engagement or a reading. In the United States authors are not paid for readings at bookstores.

Royalties: This wonderful word describes income received by authors from money earned from the sales of the book. Royalties are sent to you either by your agent or publisher. A POD author does draws royalties from the publisher in lieu of advances for books purchased by others, not copies bought by the author..

Stipends: A stipend is money paid to you for conducting a workshop, symposium, or short academic course and may not covered by a "W" declaration and withholdings.

If the total is a large amount, your tax preparer should consider transferring some of your expenses to Schedule E from Schedule C to offset the additional income.

The final total—either *net income or net operating loss*—is transferred to the front of the 1040 form on line 17.

Net Operating Loss (NOL)

When your expenses exceed your income, it is a

Writing as a Small Business

net operating loss or NOL. This negative sum is not lost, but it is applied against other income on the front page of the 1040 – Line 17 to calculate your total income. Most authors with depreciation, home business and small business consideration will have a net operating loss, even if they have substantial income from the sale of their publications. This is where careful record-keeping pays off when you utilize the Schedule C for operating your authorship as a small business.

June Walker in *Self-Employed Tax Solutions,* on p. 13, quotes a court ruling to the extent that profits are not immediate in the creative field. It discusses the intent of serious people to make a profit. This is the summation of the court ruling:

> Dec. 25, 804
> "It is well recognized that profits may not be immediately forthcoming in the creative art field. Examples are legion of the increase in value of a painter's works after he receives public acclaim. Many artists have to struggle in their early years. This does not mean that serious artists do not intend to profit from their activities. It only means that their lot is a difficult one. . . ."
> Sebastian de Garzia and Anna Marie de Garzia v. Commissioner Docket No. 89974, Tax Court Memorandum Decisions. 1962-296.

The court stresses that the tax payer must prove

his or her intent to make a profit, even if it is a long time coming. Jodi Picoult commented in *Writer's Digest* that her "overnight success" was a long night, which lasted 15 years.

Watch for mistakes—double check your math.

It is easy to transpose numerals when entering them in your spreadsheet. Check them against your receipts after posting; several days later is a good lag.

I was standing in front of a GED class, demonstrating how to calculate the perimeter of a rectangle—add the lengths of the four sides. A flash of memory occurred from 30 years prior to that evening. In 1965, I purchased a farm and figured the line fencing for depreciation. But instead of adding two lengths and two widths, I had multiplied the length times the width. My tax preparer noticed the high value and reduced it to some extent, but it was still outrageous. The math error went through all of those audits until it was depreciated out and was never discovered by the IRS auditors. After 40 years I hope the statute of limitations has expired on that mistake.

Withholdings or Quarterly Tax Payments.

Authors generally have a job that produces the major part of their income when they begin writing. P.D. James completed the years required for her to draw retirement from her employer, even though

Writing as a Small Business

she had ten international best-sellers and a BBC televison series to her credit.

Withholdings are declared on the "W" forms, W2 being the most familiar, but they run through W9. Dan Poynter suggests, in *Self-Publishing Manual* on p. 103, making adjustments to your W2 withholdings to give yourself more disposable income in anticipation of a net operating loss.

We do the opposite and over-withhold. There was a time, when interest rates were high, that your money could work better for you than being held in escrow by the IRS. This is not true in today's economy. Our checking account earned less than $30 for 2006. By following this method, even in the fat-interest years, and with help from some understanding bankers, we managed to pay for three farms with yearly installments when we received our tax refund.

> Congress writes and passes huge laws creating federal agencies then gives to the agency the right to draw up the rules and regulations as to its operation and administration that have the force of law. We use the term 80% rule, but it may not be written in the law that created the current IRC. It may have been issued as a regulation. Then there are changes every time a court ruling occurs or a letter is issued from the IRS in response to a query. These nuisances are the responsibility of the tax preparer, so **be very careful to obtain someone who keeps current**. A computer generated program like Turbo Tax for the said tax year will kick it out if it doesn't conform to the current Code but it doesn't explain the reason for doing so.

We do not want to be bothered with filing quarterly estimated income tax deposits, so we claim no deductions on our W-2s and have an extra amount withheld. **If you don't have it, you don't miss it.** Let the company or the retirement system's bookkeeper do some of your work for you.

Then, unless you, win the lottery or get a huge advance, you are covered under the prepaid 80% rule. **If you do not prepay 80% of taxes owed prior to filing your return you incur a penalty.**

There is a small kicker in this one: "Prior to

filing" for many tax payers means before April 15. *It doesn't* in the case of deposits. If you know you don't have enough on deposit for the tax year to meet the 80% rule, you can submit the funds before January 31 of the calendar year following the taxable year.

Deposit the necessary funds to be credited to your account before the January 31 deadline. The money is not going to grow appreciably in your interest-bearing checking account with a rate of .075%. The penalty rates are much higher for not doing so, and having an argument with a computer is impossible.

Calculating Your Spreadsheet

At the end of the calendar year when you have all of your figures and footnotes in the correct rows and columns, you must calculate your figures.

The following is the operation for Microsoft Works 7.0, which we are using. Other programs may be slightly different. Check your manual or "help" page.

> Help for the footnotes: When you set up your spreadsheet, about line four or five type in the date 12/31/2008. Then each time you added a new entry, highlight the row and insert a new row for your entry above the December 31 date. This will help to keep your footnotes in good order below your column entries. Place the footnotes five to seven rows below the December date.

This is going to look different from the traditional addition of a column of figures. **Remember the footnotes you placed below the columns for one-time yearly expenses;** you don't want to get their amounts accidently mixed up with your other expenses.

Go to the row directly below your column names and insert a blank row, and in the "Date" column put January through December (Jan-Dec). In the next column, under "ITEM" put TOTALS – 2008.

Then scroll down to the last item you entered for the calendar year. On the extreme left-hand side of the spreadsheet, find the row number and jot it on a slip of paper. Then go back to the beginning to the blank row. It should be row two.

Move the cursor over to the first column you want to total; if you followed our scheme it will be Column D—Mileage. Move the cursor up to the toolbar and click on the little calculator.

Writing as a Small Business

The Easy Cal screen will open. Choose the first operation, "ADD," and click. A second screen will appear: Below the instructions is the word "Range" with a blank space where the cursor will be flickering. **Set your "caps lock" key.** Then enter the letter of the column followed by the row numeral where you want to begin the calculation. Next type a colon followed by the letter of the column and the row number where you want your calculation to end.

Example: D3:D150

Then click on "Next." The final screen will show where the calculation is to be posted. Then click "Finish." For Microsoft Works 7.0 these calculation formulas must be set individually in each cell of the "Total" row.

Before freezing your entries (the instructions are located under FORMAT for our spreadsheet), carefully check all of your entries against your receipts and notebook. You may discover a trip to the post office or other expense you failed to enter. Find the appropriate row and insert a blank row for the missed entry. You will need to reset your calculation formula to accommodate the added entry for each column. Do the checking first before totaling your columns.

Make two or three paper copies when you are satisfied with the sheet. *You cannot print a copy of a frozen spreadsheet from most programs.* When you have sufficient paper copies and have carefully checked your postings for accuracy, then follow the program's directions to freeze the work and save it to a read-only CD.

Better check: You may have to save it to the read-only CD before you do your freezing operation. Different programs operate in different fashions.

You can take the entire spreadsheet to your tax preparer, but we make 5x8 cards with each expense listed. It helps save him from shuffling through excess paper. One of the extra copies should go in your file in your accountant's office. This is especially true if you give your tax preparer permission to handle any inquires on your behalf from the Internal Revenue Service.

Word File: Accounting Outline of Procedures

IF Publishing. Using Microsoft 7.0 Spreadsheet

Columns for Spreadsheet – to be reported on Schedule C of 1040 Internal Revenue U.S. Individual Income Tax Return, its supporting forms, and Schedule E.

Spreadsheet file is utilized and saved frequently to the desktop and auxiliary disks with the "make a duplicate copy" slot marked.

A – Date
B – Item
C – Check Number

Writing as a Small Business

D – Mileage
E – Direct Sales
F – Sales Tax Collected
G – Royalties, Advances, Grants & Gratuities to be declared on Schedule E
H – Books used for Advertising
I – Advertising
J – Commissions
K – Interest on designated credit card and other business loans.
L – Legal & Professional Fees
M – Office Expense
N – Supplies

Small equipment, under $500 are used as an expense; larger amounts are moved to Form 4562 for Depreciation and Amortization.

Small repairs under $50.00 are declared; larger amounts are accounted for on Line 21 of Schedule C.

For columns "M" and "N" follow the rule of prepositions

If the expense was acquired:

"To" operate the business it is entered under "M" for Office Expenses;

"In" the operation of the business it is entered under "N" for Supplies.

O – Taxes & Licenses
    Sales Taxes Paid
    Retail Sales Permit or License – costs of obtaining.

Permits for trade shows & book fairs, etc.

P – Travel & Lodgings

Overnight away from "tax home" meals are fully deductible as travel expenses.

Q – Meals & Entertainment

Full amount recorded but only 50% can be claimed.

R – Merchandise Purchased

S – Publishing Expenses

T – Editing and Research Materials

U – Utilities – utilized on form 8829

FOOTNOTES for large yearly expenses for accounting on supplemental attachments to Schedule C.

Form 4562 – Depreciation and Amortization

Form 8829 – Expenses for Business Use of Your Home

NOTES

Incidental information that facilitates tax preparation and state sales tax information.

Total square footage of home – square footage of space devoted to business – percentage the business occupies (carry this information over from year to year

Value of home and the method by which it is calculated. Add major repairs or property improvements to this figure.

Might consider keeping a running record of the

amount depreciated each year with the year. This will help with Schedule D if you sell your home later. The figures will be available on your spreadsheet.

Integrity of records – Final records are first frozen on the spreadsheet to prevent tampering after duplicate copies are made. They can be stored on a read-only CD and placed in a safe deposit box. Keep the operating system by which the transfer was made if you upgrade or change systems so the CD can be read at a later date. Paper records are maintained for three years.

A sample copy of the spreadsheet is included on the following pages for your convenience.

Nash Black

2004	Item	C#	Milage	Direct Sales	Sales Tax Col	Advances Roy	Books for Ads	Advertising	Commissions	Int. on CC
J-D	TOTALS		494	1202	14	45	3	75	10.5	25
1-2	Morgan San. Garbage --									
1-4	Book -- Bar guide		93							
1-5	UPick Press									
1-6	Woods Supplies									
1-9	H.Market-backrest									
1-9	Phone & Internet									
1-10	Library-Research		16							
1-11	Book Signing			230	14					
1-11	RECC -- BD									
1-12	JB Bookstore			525					10.5	
1-12	Blue Moon Credit	580				45				
1-14	Books for Review						3			
1-15	Star -- Ad in Prog.							75		
1-18	Tax Preparation	583	52							
1-18	Sales Tax Paid for 2003									
1-19	J-town Water-BD									
1-26	Office Depot		93							
1-27	Hoilday Inn									
1-27	Blue River WriterC	589	240	447						25
1-29	Publishers Press									
1-30	Foss Jordan -- Edit	636								
12-31										
12-31	End of Accounting Year									

FOOTNOTES

12-30 59 books left in inventory
11-9 Property Taxes on 4752 New View Road for 2004 -- C# 1420 -- 856.46
8-9 Insurance on 4752 New View Road for 2004/2005 -- C# 1380 -- 978.70
3-20 Homestead Computers -- HP Laptop -- $1900

NOTES

4751 New View Road   2400 sq. ft.
Value (PVA, Like Property, Improvements) --
$250,000 - $9,500 lot = $240,500

HomeOffice- 523 sq. ft. - 23%
*note for sales tax books sold with no tax due $520
Sales tax collected sales -- $608.70
Sales tax Collected -- $42.30

Writing as a Small Business

2004	Item	Legal & Prof Fees	Office Expense	Supplies	Taxes & Licenses	Travel & Lodgings	Meals & Entertain.	Books Pur.	Publishing Expenses	Editing & Research	Utitlities
J-D	TOTALS	80	183	49	341	170.51	63.4	340	800	501.25	347.1
1-2	Morgan San. Garbage --										36
1-4	Book -- Bar guide									1.25	
1-5	UPick Press								800		
1-6	Woods Supplies			49							
1-9	H.Market-backrest		51								
1-9	Phone & Internet										83
1-10	Library-Research										
1-11	Book Signing										
1-11	RECC -- BD										205.19
1-12	JB Bookstore										
1-12	Blue Moon Credit										
1-14	Books for Review										
1-15	Star -- Ad in Prog.										
1-18	Tax Preparation	80									
1-18	Sales Tax Paid for 2003				341						
1-19	J-town Water-BD										22.91
1-26	Office Depot		131								
1-27	Hoilday Inn					170.51	63.4				
1-27	Blue River WriterC		0								
1-29	Publishers Press							340			
1-30	Foss Jordan -- Edit		0							500	

Travel/Expense/Activities Journal

While working on *Writing as a Small Business*, it dawned on us that things were piling up at a rapid rate. To quote a line from *Travelers*, our Christmas story: *"The ball kept getting bigger and going faster and faster."* The same was true of our writing career; we were juggling the promotion of *Qualifying Laps, Sins of the Fathers* and *Taxes, Stumbling Blocks and Pitfalls for Authors 2007*— books we had previously published. At the same time *Travelers* was in the final edit process and the next Brewster County story was developing to the point of submission to a professional editor as we began the research necessary for a fourth mystery.

We needed a way to keep track of our activities and expenses. The small notebook wasn't fulfilling our specific needs for greater organization and record keeping, with the inclusion of notes.

We started keeping a journal file of our daily activities to reside on our desk top, in plain view when we boot up or close the computer. Your work habits will let you know as to whether entries need be made daily or weekly, if you should include a journal in your record keeping, but it is working for us. Like all files, we periodically save it to an auxiliary disk for safety.

Below are sample entries as they were written, rough notes that will not mean much to anyone but the individual who wrote them. For clarity and to make things easy to see, we enter milage and

Writing as a Small Business

monetary amounts in red; they will correspond with the entries in our spreadsheet for further documentation of our intent to sell our books and the activities in which we engage to do so. You can color code anything that is important to you; publishing goals in blue, items for spreadsheet in red, text in black and bright ideas in yellow. The easier the information is to locate, the more useful the information in your journal becomes.

This is an excellent place to cut and paste the content of e-mails, which contain notes important to your writing career and not have them taking up valuable space in your computer. The content is up to you; it only takes a few minutes and being able to chart your time gives you a picture of your writing activities.

Sample entries
TRAVEL/EXPENSE/ACTIVITIES JOURNAL FOR IF PUBLISHING

September 4, 2007

35 miles – Russell County Arts Council meeting – sold two copies of *Sins of the Fathers*. Made arrangements for Margaret Thrasher to sell tickets for "Ghosts of Russell County" stage show where we will introduce *Travelers*.

2. Wrote a review of June Walker's *Self-Employment Tax Solutions* for Amazon.com.

September 5, 2007

20 miles – Jamestown Library got copies made of the review of *Sins* from the Times Journal published August 28th.

2. McKenny & Blair (behind the main library) paid homeowners insurance for one year

3. Health Spa – interviewed and exchanged information with Cindy Holsclaw about her work as an artist, the organization in Somerset "Society of Decorative Painters" and her experience with having her home studio visited by the IRS. Gave her a copy of the review from the TJ. She will take sample copies of *Writing as a Small Business* to Louisville for national art conference in December as the material pertains to both authors and artists.

4. Wrote a review of Diana Gabaldon's *Lord John and the Private Matter* for Amazon.com

5. E-mailed Michele Center at Outskirts Press

Writing as a Small Business

about questions pertaining to *Writing as a Small Business; Travelers* (second email) if second edits made it.

6. E-mailed Todd Wilson about possible titles for Star's new webpage and gave him information about Cindy as a possible new member of the Arts Council.

7. Ordered books from Amazon on sprint cars and Agatha Christy, Christmas story for Listamainia

8. 34 miles – Russell Springs Library – gave them 3 hardbacks (9.00) and three paperbacks (1.50) for a total donation of $10.50. – Checked on supply of *Sins* and *Laps* for sale – Check out the Time/Life *Badlands* for research on same title (possible publication/Sept. 2008)

9. Meal at the Porch – signed and left four copies of *Sins* for sale and posted a copy of the TJ review on the wall inside the front door. Talked to Connie Miller (owner) about February, 2008 book club meeting when I will be doing a program on *Sins* – Meal $17.17

10. Treasure Nook (across the parking lot from Porch) – purchased silk spider plants to hang in the window of writing area – used a parrot willow catch pot and macrame hanger Marilyn Bennington gave me years ago – looks good – $27.54.

Will your journal serve as evidence for an audit? Yes, it should at least substantiate your "intent" to make a profit, which is at the heart of Schedule C filing. Should you need to challenge the

IRS in tax court, it will be invaluable to your attorney. Tax professionals must evaluate a court action in terms of the money and time involved as to whether to fight or let it go. These economic considerations are based on the greater benefit to you, their client.

We plan to put a paper copy of our Travel/Expenses/Activities Journal in the tax documentation file—it will be there if we need it.

At this time the IRS still thinks in paper mode, although each form mentions the paper reduction law, which applies to the Bureau, not the taxpayer. Will it eventually change? Yes, but it will take time the same as electronic filing.

Chapter 7
Storing Your Records

Our spreadsheet for IF Publishing has expanded through U. We open a new spreadsheet on January 1 and close it on December 31. Being lazy before freezing the spreadsheet from the previous year we make an extra copy, rename it for the next calendar year and all the other date-sensitive areas, then delete information for the previous year and start with a clean slate. Remember to keep information in your NOTES that does not change. This saves having to spend time rebuilding a spreadsheet each year. The same is true for the word file; once it is set up, there is no need to create a new one each year, just make sure the new copies have a current date.

Check "Print Preview" to ascertain adjustments

to column width. Purchase a ream or packet of legal-size paper and run some tests prints. It is much easier to file in a permanent file if all the columns fit on the same legal-size page.

But, you might be saying, we said that we already have three computer copies. Correct, we did, but the Code requires you to keep **ALL** of your records for the three prior years. Audits still require paper copies. These include receipts, bank statements, credit card statements, travel/expense records etc. We keep them for four years as a safety measure.

You are not "innocent until proven guilty" before the IRS. *You are guilty until you prove yourself innocent, which is a reversal of the American jurisprudence system.*

We have individual file boxes with hanging divisions, and each January we take the oldest and dispose of those records. We run the paper through the shredder (especially anything that has our credit card or bank account numbers on them), then slap a new label on the front and top of the box for the new tax year. This is our supporting evidence in case of a trip to an audit.

We also have a booth in an antique mall, down from four at one time, but 9/11 and economic changes have drastically reduced our business. Until we retired, we owned and operated three farms and three rental houses. These endeavors required greater storage space for records. The change in our circumstances today demands less storage capacity, but we have them, so we use them.

You could do nicely with a business-letter-sized expandable file for storage when you first start collecting records. It would fit out of the way on a shelf in a closet. But keep those paper files and those returns; they are important.

The burden of proof is on the tax payer. So far, the IRS has spent billions trying to streamline their electronic accounting procedures, but in reality it has some gray areas where the tax payer can be enfolded in obsolete practices. Congress has been reluctant to fund any more "system up grades" that do not work. The IRS does not have the freedom of individuals "to junk it and start over" when their system does an inadequate job.

Disaster Preparedness

Think about what is easy to take on your way out of your dwelling should you be caught in a disaster. **What cannot be replaced?**

Plan—a *little mental horror imagining*—and travel light. Tape a copy of all emergency phone numbers and insurance policy numbers inside the lid of a metal file, then include auxiliary disks of your work and records, licenses and certificates, spare batteries for your cell phone, a flashlight that doesn't use batteries, sufficient collapsible blankets to protect you and yours from the elements, and power bars. Put them in a metal box and store it all near a primary exit. Get your loved ones (human and animal) out, then grab your box and run.

No one wants to think about disasters, but they happen all too frequently—both natural and man-made. Our purpose is to nudge you into creating your own emergency box, to keep it current and to keep it handy.

We write mysteries and read mysteries. The next time a hurricane makes for the Gulf Shore or East Coast, find a copy of John D. MacDonald's *Condominium*. It was published in 1977, before CNN became a part of our lives, and it will help you understand some of the jargon they use when tracking the storm. For the aftermath of Katrina, James Lee Burke's, *The Tin Roof Blowdown* is a mind-awakening experience.

More recent than the 2005 hurricane season is the 2006 firestorm that incinerated the firefighters near the West Coast. Nevada Barr's *Firestorm* contains a description of a firestorm so vivid that the sweat will run down your forehead.

Terrorist activities: Dana Stabenow's *Blindfold Game* is a strong story about the beleaguered, underfunded U.S. Coast Guard, which has the awesome responsibility of protecting our entire coast line within the five-mile limit. Another good read.

These are books we've taken from our personal shelves. There are many others. If you write, you must read, because you can safely assume that if you have a great story or a fantastic topic, someone else has been there before you. Find it, and learn what the competition is doing.

Chapter 8
Defense, Defense

When we published *Qualifying Laps*, we took a four-year-old laptop and converted it to business usage. Our website and writing-business e-mail addresses were to reside on this computer to help maintain the integrity of the ones on which we work.

No, the cost of the old machine was not an income-tax deduction. It was not purchased the year it was put into service as business equipment. It could have been under the rules for establishing a small business, but it would have entailed locating the original invoice and declaring capital assets, which we did not care to do. The new updated operating system was deductible as an expense. It was a nice try, but it did not work because the computer did not have sufficient memory to power the new operating system.

Computers change, operating systems change. I started teaching spreadsheets on Apples with 48K of memory powered by two auxiliary metal disk-drives using five-and-a-quarter-inch floppies. Charles Fought, our repairman, puts it this way: "You go to work in the morning, they are one way; by the time you go home, they have changed." A ten-year depreciation period is very optimistic.

Devices to which you save data change and slots for the older methods are not included in newer models. Most of these devices have problems: Small floppies are gone; CDs peel; auxiliary disk drives destruct; lightning strikes and power outages wipe out the entire system. At the first rumble of thunder, we unplug everything. Most problems from this source come into your home through the phone line, not the electrical service.

When you purchase a computer, you may assume it is free from problems and "hitchhikers." *Not true*. "Stuff" resides on your new computer for no other reason than that the manufacturer was paid to install it on their machines. It is like the "co-advertising" practiced by publishers, bookstores, and groceries you discovered during your market research. Call "craplets" by the industry, these little "free" programs can foul up your hard drive, slow the performance of your operating system, and can facilitate crashes.

PC World's article "20 Tools to Get the Junk

Writing as a Small Business

Off Your PC," August 27, 2007 address this problem:
www.pcworld.com/article/id,136109/article.html.
Most of the tools mentioned in the article are free downloads, but check them out before you use them. Employ some of these regularly during the life of your computer, it is your major working tool.

Clean Up Your Computer and Do It Often.

The following steps will help your computer's performance, make your life easier, and protect it against worms, viruses, and spy ware. Nothing is perfect, but you can take some precautions. You are driving on a crooked road with a sheer drop on both sides, so install your own guard rails.

1. On a regular basis, set it to defrag while you sleep.

2. Scrub your software. Use a strong security system that updates frequently. **Save everything on your computer to an outside source before you begin this procedure.**

3. What services does your Internet service provider furnish for you as a customer? There are plenty out there to choose from, except where we live, and it's the

only game in town. Ours uses McAfee, which catches viruses, pornography, advertising, and spam mail. We have it set at the highest filtration, so we can tell the service provider what to let into our box and what remains quarantined on the main server. Notices are e-mailed to us from the provider, and we check them periodically—99.9% of the time it is a mass delete.

4. E-mail: Consider having two or more accounts. One for your writing career, the link from your website, and other places that have buttons to link the browser to the author. Then create a separate account for your personal correspondence. If possible, keep your name out of your personal e-mail address. The same goes for your mother's maiden name, date of birth, driver's license, house number, etc. Anything that can be traced to you.

Ditto for passwords. Use nothing that identifies you from an easy on line search (easy for the mayhem proponents and crooks anyway). Do this especially for any online shopping; make it hard for them to find you by having a free address at Hotmail or Yahoo, which you use only for shopping.

Writing as a Small Business

Cleanup Your E-mail Box.

Empty weekly or daily the sent and delete boxes. Keep a paper copy if the e-mail is important, or create a file and move it to an auxiliary drive, such as a Memorex Travel Drive. So far, for us, this product has been dependable and it is relatively inexpensive. Another solution is to cut and paste the essential information to a word file, and delete the remainder.

Photos, cartoons, audio strips, and video files devour space. These are all potential sources of spy-ware intrusions, which are discussed later. If you must save them, move them to an external hard drive.

Do not open attachments unless you have solicited them. We seldom open e-mails with attachments—even from family members. The little paperclip is a signal to hit the delete key. Tell your friends and family you will not open attachments. Major authors inform their readers in their notes or on their Web page that they will not open attachments. Follow their style; they have learned from experience.

This technique works for Outlook Express but does not work on Yahoo or Hotmail, unless they have upgraded their service. If you are forwarding an e-mail, when you are in the forward mode, the e-mail can be edited. Go down and delete all of the e-mail addresses to which it has been sent. Then use the "bcc" notebook to the left of the "To" space to send your e-mails. All of those e-mail addresses floating around are collected and sold to advertisers and others for illegal endeavors. There is a huge underground industry that does nothing else. Your time is too limited to pay much attention to the e-mail circuit.

Virus Protection

Buy the best you can get and update, frequently. Employ several systems if you are working in cyberspace, visiting websites frequently or if you send/receive mass e-mailing from an unprotected sources. A major reviewer of print on demand books has a virus in its email account. We informed the reviewer of the problem, but we no longer subscribe to its service because it was never corrected over a period of eight months. If we want to browse new books reviewed by this source, we go in by the Internet to their website.

Phishing, Spoof, or Spam

Companies deal with Internet problems on a wholesale level. Unfortunately about all you can do is report it. For eBay send it to spoof@ebay.com and for Amazon, it is report@Amazon.com.

A scam arrived in my e-mail purported to be from **PayPal**, which is used by many Internet sites

Writing as a Small Business

to transmit payment between sellers and buyers through credit cards. I do not have an account with PayPal. PayPal addressed this right away because maintaining its integrity and security is the heart and soul of its business. PayPal reporting sites: https://www.paypal.com/wf/f=default or https://paypal.com/ewf/f=default.

Another avenue is to send it to the Federal Communications Commission www.fcc.gov; it is their business to police the communications industry. Help put these guys out of business, so everyone can enjoy the greatest international free enterprise market ever devised since the Constitution and Bill of Rights of the United States were ratified.

> Nash Black received a solicitation from a bogus charity which was followed up by a phone call. He is a Southerner and said "Excuse me" before he hung up the phone, but we expect the caller understood. It takes years of elocution training below the Mason-Dixon Line to do it correctly.

It took less than four months for direct mailers pushing credit cards to find IF Publishing while reviewers and distribution houses were ignoring *Qualifying Laps* and sending rejection slips. Call this number 1-888-567-8688; it will eventually stop some of the pre-approved credit card solicitations generated by the three credit bureaus that collect financial information about you.

A book to check out: *Scam-Proof Your Life: 377 Smart Ways to Protect You and Your Family From Ripoffs, Bogus Deals, and Other Consumer Headaches,* AARP Books/Sterling Publishing.

This one I discovered when searching for addresses of state revenue departments posted on the Louisiana Department of Revenue Web page. Friends tell me it was on TV. No one is exempt from scams, but this one has to top the list of audacity.

> Dated Dec. 8 2006
>
> "It has come to our attention that there's an e-mail scam circulating to taxpayers. People are receiving e-mail from who they believe is the **Internal Revenue Service** (IRS), Informing them that they are eligible to receive a tax refund after the "last annual calculations.""

The site gives an example of what the e-mail looks like, and this Web address has more information:

http://www.irs.gov/newsroom/article/0,,id=160334.00.html

The citizens of the United States were bilked for $52 billion dollars in 2004 alone by these schemes. The only other places we see figures of that magnitude are in our federal budget and corporate

Writing as a Small Business

financial statements. If it should happen to you, report it to the company. Obtain a new email address and credit card every two to three years as a safety measure. Cancel the old ones and send all copies through the shredder. You will need to notify your friends, family, and business associates of the change, but it is worth the effort you take to protect yourself.

Currently, there is another making the rounds claiming to be from Social Security. We forwarded, it to the Federal Communications Commission.

Snooper/Spyware.

You do not see this one like you do an email, but it can be there working away to your disadvantage, reporting all of your computer activity to a remote contact point.

It sneaks into your computer by the backdoor imbedded in downloaded programs, e-mails, music, cartoons, photos, etc. It is used to track your actions online—purchases you make, bills you pay, websites you visit etc. Think twice about installing "freebie" software unless you know the source. Virus-free does not mean spyware-free.

The most recommended anti-spyware program is Ad-Adware at www.lavasoftusa.com/software/adaware. It was free, but now charges $30/computer for a download. It is worth the price. Microsoft XP

Pro has an anti-spyware program that industry sources report does a good job.

Since we installed Ad-Adware on our computer, it has collected, quarantined, and deleted 936 units of spyware in less than one year. This is an amazing amount when you consider the limited amount of Internet browsing we do. They have wandered in via emails from friends and family.

Three others which do slightly different things are:

- **Windows Defender** – free anti-spyware – downloads from Microsoft's website. Remember, most of these programs are designed to operate on Microsoft's Internet Explorer, which comes installed along with the operating system on the majority of personal computers. Microsoft is constantly designing new products to protect consumers from security threats, pop-ups, and slow performance.
- **Bitdefender** – A free online scanner that scans your system's memory and all files and folders for viruses. This site has many articles and tips to help protect personal computer users.
- **Pcpitstop** – A free computer checkup that can detect and fix many common computer problems. It features several different tests and scans, an information

Writing as a Small Business

center and free "help" forums.

Information about these three sites came from our Internet service provider, which is a tiny mutual cooperative phone service. All of the users are also the owners, who can come marching in the door, raising the roof when something goes wrong, and the majority show up for the annual meeting. This does make a difference in the kind and type of service you receive.

Another self-protection idea: If you are interested in accessing a website that comes in by email, d**o not click from inside your e-mail**. Print it out on a scrap paper and type it in yourself or enter the site from a Web browser. The "https" at the beginning of the Web address indicates it is a secure site.

Chapter 9
Hitting the Road and Selling

You have all your ducks in a row. You have written your novel, set up your expense spreadsheet, started collecting your records and instituted safeguards to protect your computer and records. Now the book is published and you realize you are not going to get help from your publisher in the area of marketing. Very few authors rate a book-signing tour or automatic distribution to bookstores; you must do the promotion yourself. This is where your previous market research proves valuable.

The industry standard is that you spend 10% of your work time writing your book and 80%

marketing it; the other 10% is devoted to keeping records of what you do and writing the second opus.

An excellent online site for listing your book that caters to new authors is www.OnceWritten.com. The present cost for a listing of one year is $75.

Book Signing – a Warning

TAKE COPIES OF YOUR BOOK WITH YOU. A New York Times, May 7, 2007 article by Dick Cavett spoke to this problem. We saw it happen: The book signing was arranged, the publicity was issued, eager buyers were present, but there were no books to sell. The publishers had promised to supply the books for the signing, but they didn't deliver.

We attended **The First International Mystery Theater Festival**, held in Owensboro, Kentucky. The festival drew about 900 persons, who saw 12 plays in five days. Interspersed with the theatrical performances were workshops and book signings featuring new authors and some of the most famous names in the mystery genre. The audience was mystery lovers interested in discovering new products, but the publishers did not make the books available.

Later, listening to the pros after the fiasco, we discovered this is a frequent occurrence. They always have a few on hand as a precaution. Don't

Writing as a Small Business

leave home without an extra supply of your book in the trunk of your car. Another route would be to ship your books by UPS or the US Postal Service if you are flying; air-freight costs can break the bank.

Outskirts Press, bent over backwards to get our books to a hotel address when we were on tour. It took phone calls through an obsolete system to locate the books that Outskirts had shipped days before but which were lost in the storage room. A subsequent publication was not available for a major signing. Outsirts Press's e-mail did not reach us; too great a dependence on the computer communication can be a problem. A chain is only as strong as it weakest link.

Protecting Your Credit Card While on the Road

Credit card companies could help the problem by removing the security code on the back and sending it to you under a separate mailing, as they do with your PIN. Then they would only have to deal with people like us, who send those blank checks (included with your statement) and PINs through the shredder. We might forget and send the code through the shredder.

As fast as the door is closed on one avenue to your credit card information, another one is opened. It is too lucrative an area for crooks to ignore. We've listed a few and ways to stop them

1. Be grateful for the waitress or waiter who carries a scanner to your table to record your bill. When it travels out of your sight it can be scanned into another device and the code noted. One customer, after a few moments followed his card to the cash register. A kid was talking on a picture cell phone and transmitting a picture of the man's credit card while punching in the numbers to a recording device.
2. When the card is brought back to your table, **check to see if it is your card.** Customers have found belatedly they were victims of the "old switcheroo." They had been given an expired credit card belonging to someone else and slipped it into their billfold without looking.
3. The same thing happened at a health club when a man discovered his locker open when he thought he had locked it. He checked; everything seemed in order—nothing taken. Several days later he discovered his credit cards had been replaced by expired cards.
4. This one happened to us recently. The waitress at a small restaurant made a mistake entering our bill. She gave us a credit for the mistake and reentered the correct amount. When our monthly

Writing as a Small Business

> statement arrived—four days after the incident—the same amount of the mistake had been recharged to our credit card. We returned and asked for a new credit. Information was taken by the owner without our number. Later, we learned the manager had been arrested for embezzling. Our actions may have alerted or provided the proof necessary for the indictment.

These are examples, but there are thousands more. Be alert to the risks when using a credit card.

You are traveling on your book tour and not likely to be back in the area, which makes you a perfect victim for identity theft. These operators are slick—they employ spotters to check your license plate, follow you into a restaurant and point you out to the "scam man," or transmit a message by cell phone. Consider your liability. Credit (not a debit card) card issuers must, by law, absorb fraud over $50, but only if you report it. Always check your monthly statement.

The term "shoulder surfing" is when someone standing behind you reads the numbers off your card as you wait in line at the checkout counter. This can be also be accomplished with one of the small video phones. Keep your card hidden from view.

Take some advice from Warren Buffet: Stay away from credit cards and invest in yourself. Pay it off every month; it saves interest charges.

Traveling and Lodgings

What do you do with those hotel room cards used throughout the industry?

This "information leak" was discovered, by accident, by the Pasadena Police Department. They were conducting a symposium on identity theft at a major hotel chain. Using one of the hotel key-cards for demonstration, they discovered, imbedded in the magnetic strip not only the room number, but also the customer's home address, credit card number, and code.

When those cards are returned to the desk they are thrown in a drawer and the information remains on them until the card is given to another customer. So it's easy for someone to take some home for a little midnight shopping. Do not leave them in your room, either during your stay or when checking out; do not return them to the desk (you will not be charged for them; this is illegal); do not pitch them in the trash, either in the room or at the airport. Take them home and destroy them.

For anyone who has had to go back down to the desk for a new card when their cell phone rang too close to their "key," this is another method to destroy the information on the card. Put the card inside your cell phone and use the house phone to call your cell phone. That should wipe the information off the magnetic stip.

Were we surprised when registering at a hotel to see the above advice posted on the wall behind the desk! We don't own a cell phone and made it up for this book. Now do you see what we meant when we said, "If you think you have a great idea someone has been there before you"?

Chapter 10
Protecting Yourself, Your Family or Heirs

For many people this is the tough part of running a business and living: devising plans for the eventuality of disablement or death. Age is not a factor, because the possibility exists no matter what your age.

The first thing you need to do is clean house. Consider all the "stuff" you have been acquiring over the years of your life. The last comment page of the October 2007 *Writer's Digest* addresses this issue. You are a writer with your own business; besides getting your financial affairs in order, you need to simplify your life. Do you want to spend your time dusting or writing?

Take a hard look. Consider how much you want

to pack if you are moving. Even if moving expenses are deductible, as they are in some cases, how much do you want to move across country?

Next, consider your situation, family, friends, companions, etc., and do some hard planning. What happens if you are disabled? Who will be responsible for your care and rehabilitation? Who will assume the costs when all of your insurance is exhausted? Who will need to deal with the myriad forms for public assistance?

Most libraries have copies of generic forms, **but read them carefully**. I do not want to be saying the same thing over and over through this section but it is the same as with any contract you sign: Read it carefully and fully understand each provision. Discuss the provisions of each legal instrument mentioned with a lawyer, family, or friend who will be affected by your decisions.

Durable Power of Attorney

The first thing you need to acquire is a durable power of attorney; give the grantee a copy. Write your own, to suit your needs. Lawyers can also advise you as to the form to follow, or they will prepare one for you. "Durable" does not mean it is viable after death. The grantee cannot take any new actions in your name, only clear up old ones executed prior to your death.

Investigate the powers this legal instrument

Writing as a Small Business

conveys before you sign anything. Be comfortable with them, and **remember relationships do change**. When they do, your legal arrangements need to be revised to cover the new situation.

Living Will

Do you want to be kept alive on machines while the courts fight over the remains? Do you want to be an organ donor? Some states make provision for this procedure on the back of your driver's license—Kentucky is one.

A living will is a painless procedure and simple to execute. Consider it after the power of attorney.

Wills or Trusts

This is the point where you consider all of your possessions and how they will be distributed after your demise. You need to be very careful how you structure your bequests.

If you have children who are underage, who will be designated to assume guardianship? How will the proceeds of your assets benefit them and last long enough to pay for their education? There are many more questions to be considered; these are only examples.

This is where you must sit down with an attorney and plan for a future in which you are not around to manage for your loved ones. Under all circumstances, make sure all provisions are clearly spelled out; provide a specific numerical value for trust funds to be paid to the executor for their services. For many people a trust is a much wiser document than a simple will. Some forms of trusts avoid the probate court and avoid the draining of assets by inheritance taxes—again, this vital document must be updated as relationships change or your executor moves from the area where you reside.

We cannot emphasize strongly enough how careful you must be in this area so your assets will go to the designate and not be syphoned off as administrative fees, estate taxes, or other estate expenses. Money left in unclaimed bank accounts eventually reverts to the state if owners cannot be located by advertising in the newspaper with the largest circulation in the area.

Your will or final arrangement is a living item that must be reviewed at intervals. Don't put off making this vital document, and keep it current.

Safe Deposit Box

Your safe deposit box: Place a duplicate key and the location with a trusted source, maybe with a copy of your will in your attorney's office. Don't leave these things around where they can get lost or forgotten. States, after a period prescribed by law, open abandoned boxes and auction the contents for the benefit of the state. If you move, remember to clean it out and secure another box at your new residence. Do you have a second signature on your box? The decision is up to you.

Insurance

Business. Protecting your business is your first concern. The standard homeowner or apartment dweller policy will provide some coverage. You can also add a rider to your homeowners, specifying business coverage on the dedicated portion of home occupied by your small business, or you can take out additional coverage through a separate policy. Insurance coverage is a question the small-business owner must evaluate against the amount of investment in his or her supplies, furniture, equipment, reference library and other business tools.

Personal. How much insurance is necessary to provide for your funeral and burial or cremation? Check with a mortuary for details and make your decision. Do you have small children? Estimate their expenses through college. Are the proceeds paid directly to the beneficiary or into a previously established trust?

Term life insurance costs the least, and today it does provide some return premiums to the policy holder. Amounts can be staggered to cover different life styles and responsibilities.

See a reputable insurance agent, develop

scenarios and get quotes. The Internet has many of these services, but we stand on the side of a local representative; it is much easier to make changes, not to mention the quality of service.

Elder-care insurance. Medicare does not (at this time) provide for nursing home care. As our population ages, this is another insurance vehicle to investigate.

Making Mistakes

We've told you several of ours. The "school of hard knocks" is a rough tutorial. The simplest answer is yes, you will make mistakes. If you don't, then you need to get busy, because you are not working hard enough to write the best book you can and merchandising it to sell.

> One of the treasured letters we have from the IRS illustrates this idea. We got a notice of unreported income. One item was our Social Security which was listed right on the front page of our return. The other was a withdrawal from a Tax-Free mutual fund. The TF abbreviation from the 1099-B didn't cross-reference with tax free in their estimation. We made copies of the documents and sent them back. Their response was a full page letter, which in essence said we made a mistake, but are not about to admit it was an error.

Writing as a Small Business

We are not sure what frightens people so much about admitting a mistake, but it is impossible to correct it until you do. There is no crime involved in saying "I blew it." There is also no reason to use it as a crown of thorns to beleaguer yourself and bore your friends and family.

Go to work and correct the error. What is the use of making a mistake if you don't benefit from the action?

Taxes, Stumbling Blocks and Pitfalls for Authors 2007 was a mistake; it had major flaws and some very good points for financial considerations by beginning authors. It is difficult to tell from a manuscript where the flaws lie until you hold the finished book in your hands. We made a big mistake and yes, it will cost us, but we intend to earn the respect our work deserves, so we did more reading and research.

Writing as a Small Business is the result of a complete rewrite—an excellent reason to use a POD publisher. You can correct your mistakes, then move on to the next level of your ability.

A famous author expressed it in this fashion; You don't care enough about your work or yourself when you allow a mistake to stand. Although I did read somewhere that you pay more dearly for a mistake than you do for a crime. Okay, authors must be able to see all sides of an issue.

Marketing with Style

As a new author, especially if you are using self-publishing or a print on demand, you will face formidable obstacles. It is very difficult, if not impossible, to get a good review for your book. Most libraries have selection policies, and if a book has not been reviewed, they cannot purchase the volume for their collection. A no-win situation, and I've written a few of those library policies.

The chain bookstores also have blanket policies against allotting shelf space to self-published books. Bob Mayer, in the *Novel Writer's Toolkit,* speaks to this issue on page 221. One follows the other, just as when you line up a set of dominos on their ends and push the last one, they all fall in line. In publishing, as in libraries, there are very few risk-takers, though they talk a good game.

I attended a workshop near the end of my library career on risk-taking. The presenter had no basic concept of what "risk-taking" involved. I couldn't help it; I started laughing. The presenter asked me what I thought was so funny, so I told her.

In 1965, in the course of one weekend, I took $250 out of a retirement system, bought a farm, bought a house through FHA, had my bank president write my credit report, and traded my 1960 Bonneville in on a new pickup truck. Then I packed my belongings and moved to another state on the strength of a verbal one-year contract for $5000, committing the cardinal sin of being a single female.

Writing as a Small Business

If you've got a good product and faith in yourself, you can make it, but it will take perseverance, a strong sense of humor and the ability to take risks—especially when you are not aware they are risks.

Develop your marketing techniques accordingly. As Joe Konrath says become "market savvy." Find your own way to sell and promote your work, but under no circumstances give up. You must go where the herd isn't feeding if you don't want to starve.

We followed Benjamin Franklin's example. He made sure he had earned sufficient resources to sustain himself and his family before he set forth to indulge in politics.

We've given you a pattern to follow so you can at least keep your head above water as you indulge in your love of writing and market your work with the "intent" of making a profit.

The area of taxes is one where we do rank as knowledgeable, having survived more than one audit. Why were we being audited so frequently? As we said in the beginning, we have no idea. The audits continued until one IRS auditor asked the first question you are supposed to be asked in an audit: "Have you ever been audited before?"

When I answered, "Yes, this is the seventeenth time." He returned, "This is ridiculous; there is nothing wrong with your return." That ended our saga, but we still keep very careful records and submit them to our tax preparer in IRS accounting form.

Learn to keep more of the money you earn, and designate your refund check to financing greater efforts to market and promote your book. You could term it recycling in the grand manner.

Appendix I
Self-Employment Taxes

Self- Employment Taxes are filed on Schedule SE.

Self-Employment taxes are levied on small business owners in lieu of withholdings for Social Security and Medicare. *They are not considered in this work,* but below is a brief explanation of how they are calculated.

This tax is levied on the **net-income** of a small business in excess of $400. Net-income or net-loss is the final figure on the Schedule C after all expenses—including final totals from the two supplements, Forms 8829 & 4562, have been subtracted from the gross income of the business entity. It is the famous bottom line.

If the net income is $400 or more, it is

discounted by 92.35% for 2006. This figure is then used to calculate the Self-Employment Tax and Medicare payments.

> Example: X Business has a *net income* of $2300. $2300 is multiplied by .9235 for a total of $2124. The $2124 is the amount on which the Self-Employment Tax & Medicare percentages are calculated.

For the year 2006 the Social Security rate was 12.9 percent with a ceiling of $94,200 of the net-income of a small business. The rate for Medicare was 2.9 percent which applies to all net earnings; **there is no ceiling**. Always check for a change in rates, your tax professional will have the current figures. The rate for medicare has increased for several years.

A deduction of one-half of the Self-Employment Tax is granted to the individual on page one of the 1040 Form as an adjustment to gross income. This lowers the ceiling for some itemized personal deductions, such as health care costs.

Appendix II

States and Their Revenue Departments for a Retail Sales Tax License

Information as to the amount of the sales tax was taken from *The World Almanac and Book of Facts 2007*.

Alabama (AL) – 4.0% – Alabama Department of Revenue, 50 North Ripley Avenue, Montgomery, AL 36132, www.alabama.gov

Alaska (AK) – nst – Anchorage www.state.ak.us

Arizona (AZ) – 5.6% – Arizona Department of Revenue, Taxpayer Information and Assistance, P.O. Box 29086, Phoenix, AZ 85038-9086 www.az.gov or www.azdor.gov/brochure/610/pdf-

Arkansas (AR)– 6% – Arkansas Department of Finance and Administration, Joel Y. Ledbetter Building, Room 2460, P.O. Box, Little Rock, AR 72203 www.state.ar.gov

California (CA) – 7.25% – California Franchise Tax Board, P.O. Box 942840 Sacramento, CA 94240-0040 www.state.ca.gov

Colorado (CO) – 2.9% –Colorado Department of Revenue, 1375 Sherman Street, Denver, CO 80261 – www.colorado.gov ph: 303 - 238 - 7378

Connecticut (CT) – 6.0% – Connecticut Revenue Services, 25 Sigourney St., Hartford, CT 06106-5032 www.ctbounb.org

Delaware (DE) – nst – Dover www.delaware.gov

Florida (FL) – 6.0% – Florida Tax Payer Services, Florida Department of Revenue, 1379 Blounstown Hwy., Tallahassee, FL 32304-2716 www.myflorida.com
http://doc.myflorida.com/dor/taxes/

Georgia (GA) – 4.0% – Georgia Department of Revenue, 1800 Century Blvd., N.E., Atlanta, GA 30345-3205 www.georgia.gov

Hawai'i (HI) – 4.0% – Hawaii Department of Taxation, General Excise License Application, P.O. Box 1425, Honolulu, HI 96806-1425 www.hawaii.gov – note: HI does not have a sales tax, but a general excise tax of 4% assessed on all business activities.

Idaho (ID) – 5.0% – Idaho State Tax Commission, P.O.

Writing as a Small Business

Box 56 Boise, ID 83756-0056 www.state.id.us

Illinois (IL) – 6.25% – State of Illinois, 101 West Jefferson Street, Springfield, IL 62702 www.illinois.gov

Indiana (IN) – 6.0% – Indiana Department of Revenue, Department of Revenue, 100 N. Senate Street, Indianapolis, IN 46204 www.in.gov

Iowa (IA) – 5.0% – Hoover Building, Taxpayer Services/4th Floor, 1305 E. Walnut, Des Moines, Iowa 50319 http://www.state.ia.us/tax/index.html

Kansas (KS) – 5.3% – Kansas Department of Revenue, Sales Tax, 915 S.W. Harrison St., Topeka, KS 66625-5000 www.accesskansas.org

Kentucky (KY) – 6.0% – Kentucky Department of Revenue, 200 Fair Oaks Drive, Frankfort, KY 40601 www.kentucky.gov

Louisiana (LA) – 4.0% – Louisiana Department of Revenue, 617 North Third Street, Baton Rouge, LA 70802 www.revenue.louisianna.gov

Maine (ME) – 5.0% – Maine Revenue Services, P.O. Box 9119, Augusta, ME 04332-1065 www.state.me.us

Maryland (MD) – 5.0% – Maryland State Department of Assessments & Taxation, 301 West Preston Street, Baltimore, MD 21201-2395 www.maryland.gov

Massachusetts (MA) – 5.0% – Massachusetts Department of Corporation and Taxation, Sales and Use Tax Bureau, P. O. Box 7010, Boston,

MA 02204 www.mass.gov

Michigan (MI) – 6.0% – Michigan Department of Treasury, Lansing, MI 48922 www.michigan.gov

Minnesota (MN) – 6.5% – Minnesota Department of Revenue, Mail Station 4410 St. Paul, MN 55146-4410 www.state.mn.us

Mississippi (MS) – 7.0% – Office of the Mississippi State Treasurer, P.O. Box 138, Jackson, MS 39205 www.ms.gov

Missouri (MO) – 4.225% – Missouri Department of Revenue, 301 W. High St., P.O. Box 311, Jefferson City, MO 65105-0311 www.state.mo.us

Montana (MT) – nst – Helena www.state.mt.us

Nebraska (NE) – 5.5% – Nebraska Department of Revenue, Nebraska State Office Building, 301 Centennial Mall S., P.O. Box 94818, Lincoln, NE 68509-4818 www.nebraska.gov

Nevada (NV) – 6.5% – Nevada Department of Taxation, 1550 College Parkway, Carson City, NV 89706 www.nv.gov

New Hampshire (NH) – nst – Concord www.state.nh.us

New Jersey (NJ) – 6.0% – State of New Jersey, New Jersey Division of Taxation, P.O. Box 281, Trenton, NJ 08695-0281 www.state.nj.us

New Mexico (NM) – 5.0% – New Mexico Regulations & Licensing Dept., 2550 Cerrillos Road, Santa Fe, NM 87504 www.state.nm.us

New York (NY) – 4.0% – New York State Department of Taxation and Finance, Sales Tax Bureau, W.A. Harriman State Office Campus,

Writing as a Small Business

Albany, NY 12227 www.state.ny.us

North Carolina (NC) – 4.5% – North Carolina Department of Revenue, 301 N. Wilmington Street, Raleigh, NC 27604 www.nc.gov

North Dakota (ND) – 5.0% – North Dakota Tax Department, 600 E. Boulevard Avenue, Bismark, ND 58505-0599 www.discovernd.com

Ohio (OH) – 5.5% – Ohio Department of Taxation, 4485 Northland Ridge Road, Columbus, OH 43229 www.ohio.gov

Oklahoma (OK) – 4.5% – Oklahoma Tax Commission, Ad Valorem Division, P.O. Box 53248, Oklahoma City OK 73152-3248 www.ok.gov

Oregon (OR) – nst – Salem www.oregon.gov

Pennsylvania (PA) – 6.0% – Commonwealth of Pennsylvania, Department of Revenue, Bureau of Trust Fund Taxes, Dept. 289901 Harrisburg, PA 17128-0901 www.state.pa.us

Rhode Island (RI) – 7.0% – Rhode Island Division of Taxation, One Capitol Hill, Providence, RI 02908 www.state.ri.us

South Carolina (SC) – 5.0% – South Carolina Department of Revenue, Sales Tax Return, Columbia, SC 29214-0101 www.sc.gov

South Dakota (SD)– 4.0% – South Dakota Department of Revenue, 445 East Capitol Ave., Pierre, SD 57501-3185 www.state.sd.us

Tennessee (TN) – 7.0% – Tennessee Department of Revenue, 500 DeaderickStreet, Nashville, TN 37242, ph: 615-253-0600, www.tn.gov/revenue,

Texas (TX) – 6.25% – Texas Comptroller of Public

Accounts, 111 E. 17th Street, Austin, TX 78774-0100, 1-800-252-5555 -- 512-463-4600 (Austin number) www.state.tx.us

Utah (UT) – 4.75% – Utah State Tax Commission, 210 North 1950 Street Salt Lake City, UT 84134-3310 www.utah.gov

Vermont (VT) – 6.0% – Vermont Department of Tax, P.O. Box 547 Montpelier, VT 05601, ph. 802–828-3261 www.vermont.gov

Virginia (VA) – 5.0% – Virginia Department of Taxation, P.O. Box 1115, Richmond, VA 23218 www.virginia.gov

Virginia Department of Taxation 804-367-8031 Business Sales & Use Tax Department 804-367-8037 directs you to www.tax.virginia.gov

Washington (WA) – 6.5% – Washington Department of Revenue, P.O. 47478, Olympia, WA 98504-7478 www.access.wa.gov

West Virginia (WV) – 6.0% – West Virginia Department of Revenue, State Capitol Room W-300, 1900 Kanawha Blvd. East Charleston, WV 25305, ph. 304–558-0211 www.wv.gov

Wisconsin (WI) – 5.0% – Wisconsin Department of Revenue, 2135 Rimrock Rd., Madison, WI 53713 www.wisconsin.gov

Wyoming (WY) – 4.0% – Wyoming Department of Revenue, Herchler Bldg., 2nd Floor West, Cheyenne, WY 82002-0110 www.state.wy.us

District of Columbia (DC) – 5.75% – Office of Tax and Revenue, 941 North Capitol Street NE, Washington, DC 20002 www.dc.gov

Bibliography

BOOKS

Applegate, Jane, *Succeeding in Small Business: the 101 toughest problems and how to solve them*, A Plume Book, c. 1982.

Bartlett, John, *Familiar Quotations: A collection of passages, phrases and proverbs traced to their source in ancient and modern literature*, 14th edition, Revised and Enlarged, Little, Brown and Company, 1968.

Commerce Clearing House, Inc., <u>Tax Court Memorandum Decisions</u>, Dec. 25, 804 (M) Sebastian de Grazia and Anna Maria de Grazia v. Commissioner, Docket No. 89972. .T.C. Memo, 1962-296. Filed December 18, 1962, p. 1572.

Ernst & Young's Tax Guide for 2007 by the Tax Partners and Professionals of Ernst & Young LLP, Peter W. Bernstein, Ed., CDS Books, 22nd ed., 2006.

Fess, Philip E. and Carl S. Warren, *Accounting Principals*, 14th ed., South-Western Publishing Co., Cincinnati, Ohio, 1984.

Francisco, Albert K. and Kenneth E. Smith, *Auditing*, 1989-90 ed., CPA Examination Review Series, Professional Publications, Inc., 1988.

CPA Exam Questions on Business Law, CPA Examination Review Series, Professional Publications, Inc, 1987.

J.K. Lasser's Your Income Tax 2006, Prepared by the J.K. Lasser Institute, 69th ed., John Wiley & Sons, Inc., New York, 2005.

J.K. Lasser's Your Income Tax 2007, Prepared by the J.K. Lasser Institute, 70th ed., John Wiley & Sons, Inc., New York, 2006.

Citation scheme: chapter.section:page number

Authors, self-employed – 9.11:232-33, 9.12:233, 40.9:631, 45.6:696

Royalty income & deductions – citations that apply to authors

Backup withholding – 26.11:480

Deducting tax preparation fee for reporting on Schedule E 19.16:394

Earned income – 36.2:585, 45.6:696

Examples – 9:11:232-233

Records to keep – p. 707 – (a chart) you need to

have a 1099-MISC for supporting evidence of income – one will be sent to the IRS from the payee.

Reference to writers in the index does not apply to authors but to a stock market technique.

J.K. Lasser's 1001 Deductions and Tax Breaks 2007: Your Complete Guide to Everything Deductible, John Wiley & Sons, 2006.

Kaplan, Martin S., *What the IRS Doesn't Want You to Know: A CPA reveals the tricks of the trade,* Ninth Edition, John Wiley & Sons, Inc., 2004

Kennedy, Michael B., Karl T. Weger, and Mark T. Nash, *PricewaterhouseCoopers 2007 guide to tax and financial planning including analysis of the 2006 tax law changes,* John Wiley & Sons, 2007.

Levine, Mark, *The Fine Print of Self-Publishing: the Contract & Services of 48 Major Self-Publishing Companies,* 2006.

Mayer, Bob, *The Novel Writer's Tool Kit; a guide to writing great fiction and getting it published,* Writer's Digest Books, Cincinnati, OH, 2003.

McFedries, Paul, *The Complete Idiot's Guide to Creating a Web Page & Blog,* 6th ed., ALPHA, 2004.

McNamara, M. Frances, *2,000 Famous Legal Quotations*, Aqueduct Books, Rochester, NY, 1967.

Nissenbaum, Martin, Barbara J. Raasch and Charles L. Ratner, *Ernst & Young's Personal Financial*

Planning Guide, 5th ed., John Wiley & Sons, 2004.

Orman, Suze with Linda Mead, *You've Earned It, Don't Lose It: Mistakes you can't afford to make when you retire*, Newmarket Press, 1994.

Parson, Mary Jean, *Managing the One-Person Business*, Dodd, Mead, & Company, New York, 1987.

Poynter, Dan, *Self-Publishing manual: How to Write, Print and Sell Your Own Book*, 15th ed., Para Publishing, Santa Barbara, CA, 2006.

Sampson, Brent, *Publishing Gems: Insider Information for the Self-Publishing Writer*, Outskirts Press, Inc., Denver, CO, 2005.

Sander, Peter, *The Everything Personal Finance Book: Manage, budget, save, and invest your money wisely!*, Adams Media Corporation, Avon, MA, 2003.

Schomp, Virginia, *How to be an Informed Investor: Protect your money from schemes, scams & frauds*, The North American Securities Administrators Association and The Council of Better Business Bureaus, Inc., Mega-Books with The Benjamin Company, Inc., 1997.

2006 Guide to Literary Agents, Kathryn S. Brogan, ed., assisted by Robert Lee Brewer and Joanna Masterson, Writer's Digest Books, Cincinnati, OH, 2005.

Walker, June, *Self-Employed Tax Solutions: Quick, Simple, Money-Saving, Audit-Proof Tax and Recordkeeping Basics for the Independent*

Professional, The Globe Pequot Press, Guilford, CT, 2005.

Weltman, Barbara, *Small Business Taxes 2007*, J.K. Lasser's, John Wiley & Sons, Inc., 2007.

The World Almanac and Book of Facts 2007, World Almanac Books, 2007

Magazine Articles

1. *AARP*, Kirchheimer, Sid, Scams Unmasked, Dec. 2006, p. 71 – the advice for keeping your computer clear of potential problems is excellent.

2. *American Libraries Direct,* The e-newsletter of the American Library Association. August 8, 2007 & August 22, 2007 editions.

3. *The Funshine News*, Vol. 1, No. 1, Your PC will run faster if you clean it up, p. 13, published by Bayside Media, Russell Springs, Ky.

4. *Journeys*, AAA, Bluegrass Edition, Nov/Dec. 2006 Protect Your Information, p. 8 & Term Life Insurance, p. 35

5. *Kentucky Living*, Thompson, Jim, Scam alert, Nov. 2006, p. 45.

6. *PC World,* 20 Tools to Get the Junk Off Your PC, August 27, 2007 www.pcworld.com/article/id,136109/article.html

7. *Writer's Digest* — many excellent articles over the past dozen years of our subscription.

Konrath, J.A., After the Big Sale, June 2004, pp. 32-37.

Lick, Sue Fagalde, Tax Relief, April, 2006, p. 61
Zbar, Jeffery, Of Football and Taxes, December, 2002, p. 48-49

You will notice the obscure small periodicals listed; these arrive in our mailbox, so we read them. The articles are not indexed by any services, but they have one distinct advantage—the person who wrote the article can be located by phone or mail about questionable information or confusion.

Major Publishers of Tax Information

Commerce Clearing House
John Wiley & Sons, Inc.
Prentice-Hall
Research Institute of America
Superintendent of Documents – U.S. Government Printing Office

Books and Websites for Tax Information for Authors

Block, Julian, *Tax Tips for Freelance Writers, Photographers and Artists.* www.writefromhome.com/taxtipsjblock.htm
Daily, Frederick W., *Tax Savvy for Small Business,* Nolo Press. Updates are available at: www.nolo.com.
Small Business Quickfinder Handbook. Published

annually by Quickfinder, ph. 800-520-8997.

SisterStates Tax Directory, mentioned in the text, offers tax information and links to forms for all 50 states. www.sisterstates.com.

Websites

Ad-Aware – www.lavasoftusa.com/software/adaware

Amazon.com – www.Amazon.com , Amazon.com Help Page.

Argati Data Recovery System – www.argati.com/AAAhttp://www.snopes.com/business/taxes/excise.asp

Federal Trade Commission – www.ftc.gov

IRS – www.irs.gov/

IRS Forms – this website has been redesigned to be "user friendly" -- http://www.irs.ustreas.gov/formspubs/lists/0,,id=97817,00.html once you achieve this link, mark it for favorites so you do not have to type it again. It works—I was checking between the "0,,id" to make sure I had commas not periods and ended up at the site when I clicked.

IRS Fraud Spam – http://www.irs.gov/newsroom/article/0,,id=160334.00.html

Nash Black – www.nashblack.com or e-mail brewsterco@duo-county.com

Reviews and Tax Updates – www.pennhand.com

Outskirts Press – www.outskirtspress.com

http://www.lavasoftusa.com/software/adaware

http://www.snopes.com/business/taxes/excise.asp

http://www.ftc.gov

University of Illinois Chicago – Tax Information
http://www.uic.edu/depts/lib/documents/resources/tax/federal.shtml
UIC Library — from this site you can access the current forms used by the Internal Revenue Service. The home page includes all the holdings of the library and their locations within the library.
The UIC Library site, at the top right-hand side of the home page has a link to www.AskALibrarian@oclc.org This is the finest site on the entire Internet for research, especially the tough questions. They have access to major databases not available to the

Writing as a Small Business

general public except through the local libraries and their subscription links. They worked for three days to locate the quote from Judge Hand; I remember seeing it in an accounting text twenty years ago. They provided most of the bibliographic information contained in the book on taxes and verified our sources.

The help page of Amazon.com on phishing begins with the comment, "Phishing has been around forever." The Internet itself as we know it was developed about 1987 or 1988, which makes it the same age as a current college freshman. Its growth has been phenomenal, but it has "growing pains." For the best and most accurate information you can locate, find an access to **AskALibrarian**. This outstanding web resource for research cannot be accessed directly; you must use an intermediary. The service can be found at your public library.

Other websites helpful to the business of authorship and selling.

www.fundsforwriters.com

www.oncewritten.com a great help for new authors.

Visit us at brewsterco@duo-county.com . Send any

information about taxes for writers you have located that we missed. We know there are other things we've not considered or located. We thank you for your consideration and help.

Acknowledgments

A deep and grateful **Thank You** goes to:

Ford Nashett, my husband, for giving me the time and space to write. He endured most of the audits and was delighted they are finished, but he stays prepared for the brown envelope invitation.

J.A. Konrath, author of *Bloody Mary*, *Whiskey Sour*, *Rusty Nail*, and *Dry Martini*, for his permission to use the quote from his article in Writer's Digest. He is a "business savvy" author, who writes great stories. He doesn't use cliches, he takes them and twists them until you are laughing so hard your sides ache.

John Pendleton, our tax preparer. He answers questions no matter how off the wall; his clients are farmers, small business owners and professionals. Authors are a new experience for him.

Barbara Morgan, **Morgan Real Estate**, Lexington, KY for reading our manuscript for informational details from a friend who forgot her birthday. She helped unearth many of the figures used for Ned Bookseller.

Ken Beard, **Lakeland Insurance,** Russell Springs, KY. Ken supplied the insurance estimates for Ned Bookseller. We try not to impose on our friends too often, but they are gracious and supply the answers to questions.

Mary Lina Berndt, our editor, who wields a red pen with the precision of a finely tuned Mercedes Benz engine.

Glenda York, staff of **Russell County Public Library**. She is our link to AskALibrarian. The same Thank You goes to all the other members of the staff: Fil, Tene, Jan and Mildred—you are our support.

Charles Fought, **Homestead Computers**, Jamestown, KY, who keeps everything operating and lets us know when we are beating our head against the wall trying to make an old dog do new tricks.

Michele Center of **Outskirts Press**, who emailed encouragement when we asked her if we were wasting our time with this non-fiction volume. She suggest the title and indicated some major errors in grammar. Her answers to all of our questions through five books are always helpful. She is in charge of all the blocking and setups from our WordPerfect document.

The support staff of **Outskirts Press,** who did the final editing, created the cover from our ideas,

Writing as a Small Business

and did the indexing.

A retired homicide captain who keeps us informed as to what the scam operators are using to defraud the public.

A retired computer systems designer, who tells us little tricks of the trade to make things work easier and how to avoid the unwanted.

All of the designers of state websites who were kind enough to put the name of the department of revenue and a mailing address on the websites. It is a courtesy the public deeply appreciates.

The people who staff the AskALibrarian websites, the Reference desks at state libraries, departments of revenue and public libraries when I used the old-fashion method, the telephone to obtain state sales tax information. You all are the greatest.

Members of **International Willow Collectors Society** who supplied the information about the location of the departments of revenue for their state, when it could not be located elsewhere.

Connie Miller (**The Porch**), Angelique Guthry (**Guthrie's**) Mildred Lawson (**Russell County Public Library**), Peggy Gorbandt (**Peggy's Books**) and Jerry Sampson (**J. Sampson's Antiques and Books**) Harrodsburg, KY for selling our books.

Wade Daffron, editor of the **Russell Register** and Greg Wells, managing editor of **The Times Journal** for your reviews.

The organizers of **Murder Goes South**,

Smyrna, GA for inviting us to present "Clues and Solutions From the IRS" at your writer's conference on January 26, 2008. Find Murder Goes South at www.murdergoessouth.com.

To the organizers of **The First International Mystery Festival**, in Owensboro, KY for five heavily packed days of both great mysteries and live theater. We didn't mind a slice of pizza at intermission and a bag of popcorn walking back to the hotel for dinner. A big thank you for allowing us to present "Clues and Solutions From the IRS" at the second **International Mystery Festival**, June 12-22, 2008. No mystery author or fan should miss this event: www.newmysteries.org.

Glossary

AAA – American Automobile Association

AARP – American Association of Retired Persons

Accountant – an individual who complies financial records from documents, supplied by their clients. They may or may not prepare and file federal, state, local and sales tax returns for their clients.

ALA – American Library Association

Cash basis – income and expenses are reported when they occur.

CPA – Certified Public Accountant

Disposable Income – total amount of income available to you after withholdings for Social Security, Retirement Deposits, Federal, State and Local income taxes. A common term is take-home-pay.

Double taxation – when the same income has taxes paid on it twice as with corporate taxes and taxes applied to shareholders dividends.

Gross income – the total amount of income before deductions.

IRC - Internal Revenue Code

IRS – Internal Revenue Service

LLC – Limited Liability Company

Marketing – the process of selling

Net Income or earnings (profit) -- the amount of income left when all deductions, and credits are applied against your gross income.

Net Operating Loss (NOL) – a negative balance on Schedule C if expense deductions exceed revenue.

Phishing – systems to obtain personal or financial information from unsuspecting victims. The old term was "bunko games." See Help Page on www.Amazon.com.

Print On Demand – POD – self-publishing by electronic files. The authors retain all rights to their publication, but must assume all responsibility for the final product.

Private Press – Vanity Press – the author submits his work to an independent print shop. The author must purchase the entire print run of the publication.

PSC – Personal Service Corporation

RECC – Rural Electric Cooperative Corporation.

Spoofing – Web pages or emails that are constructed to look like an authentic websites owned by another entity. Do Not Open. Delete it and clean out your delete folder. Report it the company who is being misrepresented.

Spy or Snooper ware – unseen programs embedded in music, cartoons or other programs that monitor your online activity.mailto:spoof@ebay.com.

Spy or Snooper Ware Protection – www.lavasoftusa.com/software/adaware

Tax-abatement – when a factory is exempted from paying taxes for a period of years to entice them to locate in an area to develop local employment.

Tax Home – place where a small business exists, which may be the owner's residence

Tax preparer – the individual who actually prepares the return.

Index

Ad-Aware, 125–126
advances, 66, 92–93
advertising expenditures, 69–70
Advisor, Hal, 14
Aeopagitica, 39
agents, 40–41
Amazon.com, 30
American Association of Retired Persons (AARP), 73, 77, 124
American Automobile Association (AAA), 50, 72–73
American Disabilities Act, 36
American Library Association, 29, 37, 50
Apple Computer, Inc., 118
Argati, 50–51
AskALibrarian.org, 4

Associated Press–Ipsos, 38
audits, 12–13

Barr, Nevada, 116
Beard, Ken, 34
Bennington, Marilyn, 111
Bill of Rights, 123
Bitdefender, 126
Black, Nash, 18, 60, 63, 67
Blindfold Game, 116
Bloody Mary, 8
Books for Authors on Taxes and Tax Planning, 87
book signings, 130–131
bookstore, anatomy of, 33–37
Brewster County Cookbook, 41

British Broadcasting
Corporation (BBC),
97
Buffet, Warren, 133
Burke, James Lee, 26, 116
business entities
    incorporation, 20–21
    sole proprietorship,
        19–20
    state income taxes, 19
    sub chapter S
        corporation, 20
Busted Flush, 12

Capone, Al, 18
cash basis, defined, 54
Cavett, Dick, 130
Center, Michele, 110
certified public accountant
    (CPA), 4, 9
Christy, Agatha, 111
co-advertising, defined, 32
Commerce Clearing
    House (CCH), 21
commission expenditures,
    70–71
computer security
    methods, 117–118
    cleanup, 119–120
        of e-mail box,
            121–122
    spam
        (phishing/spoof),
        122–125
    spyware (snooper),
        125–127
    virus protection, 122

Condominium, 116
Congress, 6, 21, 65, 98
Constitution of the United
    States, 6, 123
credentials, 2–4
credit card information,
    protecting, 131–133

death, 137
    durable power of
        attorney, 138–
        139
    insurance, life, 141–
        142
    living will, 139
    safe deposit box,
        140–141
    taxes and, 5
    wills (trusts), 139–
        140
direct sales, 59–60
Dirty Martini, 8
disaster preparedness and
    record keeping, 115–
    116
durable power of attorney,
    138–139

eBay, 122
e-books, 29–33
e-mail box cleanup, 121–
    122
entertainment
    expenditures, 78–79
*The Ernst & Young Tax
    Guide for 2007,* 22,
    23

expenditures, 56–57, 68–69
   advertising, 69–70
   commissions, 70–71
   entertainment, 78–79
   hobby, 47–48
   interest, 71
   journal of, 108–111
   legal and professional services, 72–73
   lodgings, 76–78
   meals, 78–79
   merchandise purchases, 80–82
   office, 73–74
   supplies, 74–75
   taxes & licenses, 75
   travel, 76–78
   see also schedule C form

Familiar Quotations, 39
family/heirs and record keeping, 14
fcc.gov, 123
Federal Communications Commission (FCC), 123, 125
Federal Housing Administration (FHA), 144
The Fine Print of Self-Publishing: the Contract & Services of 48 Major Self-Publishing Companies, 28–29
Firestorm, 116
First International Mystery Theater Festival, 10, 130
form 8829—Expenses for Business Use of Your Home, 89–90
form 4562-Depreciation and Amortization, 91
Fought, Charles, 118
Franklin, Benjamin, 145

Gabaldon, Diana, 110
"Ghosts of Russell County" (stage show), 110
Goldburg, Rube, 29
Grafton, Sue, 26
grants, 93
gratuities, 93–94
Guide to Literary Agents, 40, 59

Hampton Inn, 73
Hand, Learned, 5, 40
Helvering *v.* Gregory, 5
hobby expenditures, 47–48
Holsclaw, Cindy, 110, 111
Homeland Security, 64
Hotmail.com, 120, 121
Hurricane Katrina, 116

IF Publishing, 17–19
incorporation, 20–21
independent business professional (indie), 5

interest expenditures, 71
Internal Revenue Code
   (IRC), i, iii, 3, 47, 90
Internal Revenue Service
   (IRS) record keeping
   requirements, 14–16
International Digital
   Publishing Forum, 30
irs.gov/, 58

James, P. D., 96
Jamestown Library, 110
J.K. Lasser Institute, 21, 22
Johnson, Samuel "Dr.", 39
John Wiley & Sons, Inc., 22

Kentucky Department of
   Revenue, 66
Kentucky Humanities
   Council, 67
King, Stephen, 26
Kipling, Rudyard, 17
"Know Your Rights," 40
Konrath, Joe A., 8, 37, 40

Lakeland Insurance, 34
Lasser's Your Income Tax 2007, 23
lavasoftusa.com/software/adaware, 125
legal and professional
   service expenditures, 72–73
Levine, Mark, 28
Library of Congress, 17

life insurance, 141–142
living will, 139
lodging expenditures, 76–78
Lord John and the Private Matter, 110
Louisiana Department of
   Revenue, 124

MacDonald, John D., 116
Managing the One-Person Business, 11
market research
   agents, 40–41
   bookstore, anatomy
      of, 33–37
   e-books, 29–33
   money, 38–40
   print on demand
      (POD), 28–29
   private presses, 28
   publishing as an
      industry, 25–26
   readers, 37–38
   small presses, 27
   traditional publishers, 26–27
Mayer, Bob, 29, 144
McDonald's restaurant, 79
McKenny & Blair, 110
Meal at the Porch, 111
meal expenditures, 78–79
Medicare, 142, 147, 148
Memorex Travel Drive, 121
merchandise expenditures, 80–82

Microsoft Internet Explorer, 126
Microsoft Outlook Express, 121
Microsoft Works, 49, 99, 101, 102–105
Microsoft XP Pro, 125–126
mileage, 58
Miller, Connie, 111
Milton, John, 39
money, 38–40
Morgan, Barbara, 34
Morgan Real Estate, 34
Mystery Writers of America, 72

Nelson, Willie, 13
net-income, defined, 147
net-loss, defined, 147
net operating loss (NOL), 84, 94–96
Newberry award, 31
New York Public Library, 29
New York Times, 29, 32, 43, 92, 130
non-direct sales income, 67
notebooks and record keeping, 43–46
Novel Writer's Toolkit, 29, 144

office expenditures, 73–74
"Of Football and Taxes" (Zbar), 54
Ole Paul, the Mighty Logger, 31
OnceWritten.com, 130
On Demand Books, 29
1001 Deductions and Tax Breaks 2007: your complete guide to everything deductible, 21
"Ordinary and necessary business expenses," 6
Outskirts Press, 17, 28, 110, 131
outskirtspress.com, 30

Parson, Mary Jane, 11
Pasadena Police Department, 134
Patterson, James, 26
PayPal.com, 122–123
Pcpitstop, 126–127
PC World, 118
pcworld.com/article/id,136109/article.html, 119
pennhand.com, 88
personal record keeping, 7–9
phishing, 122–125
Picoult, Jodi, 96
Poynter, Dan, 41, 97
print on demand (POD), 28–29
private presses, 28
Publisher's Weekly, 40, 48, 67
publishing as an industry, 25–26

Publishing Gems, 41

Qualifying Laps, 2, 18, 47, 67, 117, 123
Quicken, 53
readers and marketing, 37–38
receipts, 46
record keeping
    audits, 12–13
    computer spreadsheets, 48–51
    family and heirs, 14
    hobby expenditures, 47–48
    IRS requirements, 14–16
    notebook, 43–46
    personal, 7–9
    purpose of, 6
    receipts, 46
    rejection letters, 46–47
    storage, 113–114
        disaster preparedness, 115–116
    tax professionals, 9–14
rejection letters, 46–47
report@Amazon.com, 122
Robards, Karen, 92
Rounds, Glen, 31
royalties, 66, 94
Russell County Arts Council, 110, 111
Russell Springs Library, 111
Rusty Nail, 8

safe deposit box, 140–141
sales and promotion, 129
    book signings, 130–131
    credit card information, protecting, 131–133
    travel and lodgings, 134–135
sales tax, 62–66, 149–154
Sampson, Brent, 41
Scam-Proof Your Life: 377 Smart Ways to Protect You and Your Family From Ripoffs, Bogus Deals, and Other Consumer Headaches, 124
schedule C form
    expenditures
        editing and research materials, 86–88
        publishing, 85–86
        utilities, 88
    goods sold, cost of, 82–84
    supplements to, 89
    vehicle information, 84
schedule D form, 91, 105
schedule E form, 91
    advances, 92–93

grants, 93
gratuities, 93–94
non-direct sales income, 67
royalties, 94
stipends, 94
schedule SE form, 76, 147
"Search Inside the Book" program (Amazon), 30
Sebastian & Anna Marie de Garzia *v.* Commissioner, 95
self-employed, defined, i
Self-Employed Tax Solutions: Quick, Simple, Money-Saving, Audit-Proof Tax and Recordkeeping Basics for the Independent Professional, 12, 47, 76, 110
self-employment taxes, 75–76, 148
Self-Publishing Manual, 41, 97
Self-Publishing Simplified, 41
Sins of the Fathers, 2, 60, 108, 110, 111
Sisters in Crime, 72
sisterstates.com, 19
Sister States Tax Directory, 19
Small Business Administration, 27
small business entity, 1
 see also business entities
Small Business Taxes 2007, 21
small presses, 27
snooper, 125–127
Social Security System, 92, 125, 147
"Society of Decorative Painters," 110
sole proprietorship, i, 19–20
spam, 122–125
spoof, 122–125
spoof@ebay.com, 122
spreadsheets, building, 53
 calculating, 99–102
 column designations, 61–62
  advances and royalties, 66
  check number, 57–58
  date, 55–56
  direct sales, 59–60
  mileage, 58
  review copies, 67–68
  sales tax collected, 66
 form 8829—Expenses for Business Use of Your Home, 89–90

form 4562—
Depreciation and Amortization, 91
journal, expenses, 108–111
net operating loss, 94–95
sample, 106–107
schedule D form, 91
self-employment taxes, 75–76
state sales taxes, 62–66
withholdings, 96–97
Word File, procedures for, 102–104
spyware, 125–127
Stabenow, Dana, 116
Stamp Act, 65
state income taxes, 19
state sales taxes, 62–66
Sterling Publishing, 124
stipends, 94
sub chapter S corporation, 20
supply expenditures, 74–75

taxes
credits, 21
death, 5
errors, correcting, 142–143
licenses expenditures, 75
resources for information on, 21–23
sales, 62–66, 149–154
self-employment, 75–76, 147–148
state income, 19
see also spreadsheets, building; individual forms and schedules

Taxes, Stumbling Blocks and Pitfalls for Authors 2007, iii, 2–3, 60, 77–78, 108
Tax Help for Authors as a Small Business, 88
tax professionals and record keeping, 9–14
1099 MISC form, 67, 91, 92
Thrasher, Margaret, 110
Times Journal, 110
The Tin Roof Blowdown, 116
traditional publishers, 26–27
Travelers, 2, 60, 108, 110, 111
travel & lodging expenditures, 76–78, 134–135
journal, 108–111
Treasure Nook, 111
trusts, 139–140
Turbo Tax, 74, 98

Writing as a Small Business

"20 Tools to Get the Junk Off Your PC" *(PC World)*, 118–119

United Parcel Service (UPS), 131
U.S. Coast Guard, 116
U.S. Court of Appeals, 45
U.S. District Court, 45
U.S. Federal Claims Court, 45
U.S. Individual Income Tax Return, 102
U.S. Postal Service, 48, 131
U.S. Supreme Court, 45
U.S. Tax Court, 21, 45
University of Illinois Chicago, 23

virus protection, 122

Walker, June, 12, 76, 95, 110
Wal-Mart, 44, 87
Webster's New World, 87
Whiskey Sour, 8
wills, 139–140
Wilson, Todd, 111
Windows Defender, 126
withholdings, 96–97
W9 form, 97
The World Almanac for 2007, 63
Wright-Patterson Air Force Base, 12
writer, defined, i

Writer's Digest, 8, 25, 38, 54, 137
Writer's Market, 25, 40
W2 form, 97, 98

Yahoo.com, 120, 121
Years Ago, 88
Your Income Tax 2007, 21

Zbar, Jeffery, 54